Corporate  Handbook

▼

Are you at risk?

Corporate Survival Handbook

▼

Are you at risk?

By Steve Isler

Corporate Survival Guide: Are You At Risk?
© 2002 by Steve Isler
ISBN: 0-9727189-0-7
Library of Congress Control Number: 2002096409

Additional copies of this book are available at the author's website: www.corpsurvival.com.

Printed in the United States of America by Morris Publishing,
3212 E. Highway 30, Kearney, Neb. 68847 (800) 650-7888

This book is dedicated to my family, my wife, my children, my late mother-in-law, and my late parents.

Table of Contents

▼

Acknowledgments

This book would not have been possible without the friendship and support of the many people engaged in the daily grind of Corporate America, particularly, several colleagues from previous employers who offered their insight and encouragement to pursue this effort. John, Dustin, Chuck, J.J., Tushar, Traver, Fred, and Tom: I will always cherish your involvement.

Vicki Krueger provided editorial guidance and assistance. I also want to thank Bradley McNally, the designer of my website, and graphics designers Judd Nichols and Nick Dexter.

My wife, Cheryl, and my children, Jeff and Abby, have been an invaluable source of support and strength throughout this process. I am also deeply grateful to my parents, who instilled in me a strong work ethic as well as love and respect for others.

Most important, I give all the glory for this book to Jesus Christ, who has equipped me in many ways in the writing of this book and in the direction of my life.

Introduction

Since the Industrial Revolution, we have seen the growth of full-time, permanent employment escalate in America. During the 20th century, numerous circumstances contributed to an over-abundance of workers in our nation who were dependent on an eight-to-five job. We saw soldiers coming home from two World Wars and two police actions in Southeast Asia, as well as the effects of the Great Depression on our agrarian society; they all contributed to the need for rapid economic expansion and jobs. The GI Bill helped meter the flow of these workers into an already stressed employment market, but at some point the demand for jobs became staggering. Consumerism coupled with the use of standardized parts in the manufacturing process helped create jobs to perform the continuous repetitive processes developed for manufacturing. Workers were being trained to do a continual task for a suspended period of time, thus creating the concept of employment as our fathers understood it. That industrial era strategy has proliferated up to the 21st century.

Prior to this industrial era, employment consisted of cottage industries within an agricultural-based economy. During this period, work was plentiful and jobs were everywhere; but the concept of permanent, full-time employment just did not exist.

In the last couple of decades, we have seen the transition from an industrial economy to that of a service-based economy. Manufacturing jobs drifted overseas. Women entered the American workplace at astonishing rates. Tremendous strides were made as female workers gained acceptance in corporate life. These changes have transformed the white-collar workplace.

Today, Corporate America employs between 28 million and 35 million people (depending on how you draw the line). Workers now have to come to grips with the re-emergence of this cottage industry concept based on changes in our global economy. We see this cottage industry every day in our approach to fielding professional sports teams as well as assessing blue-collar employment, such as the construction industry and the trades. During the past five years, self-employment overall has declined from 9.3 million to slightly more than 8 million. This trend is adding to the pressure of today's tight employment marketplace.

The self-employment trend seems to be buckling from pressure on several fronts. The mom-and-pop retailers as well as the professional independent consultants are feeling the pinch of reduced demand. Smaller retail operations are being affected by the likes of Wal-Mart and Home Depot, where reliance on sophisticated inventory systems and elaborate logistical procedures—in which products seem to appear on store shelves just in the nick of time—have displaced the localized specialty reseller. And since the Y2K initiatives of the late '90s, coupled with the steady decline in corporate profits, today's independent consultants and business people are at risk. With a new 1 million people in a less-than-elastic marketplace, the pressure is increasing for steady employment.

Truly, we have seen a time in history like no other. The assumed birthright of a job has drifted past us without so much as a shudder. At the turn of the 21st century, employment was near an all-time high in the United States. Much of this economic growth was fueled by technological needs. The Internet was being touted as the new economy, and Corporate America was getting ready to right one of its biggest technological debacles in history, Y2K. To complicate matters, interest rates were manipulated to the point that a false sense of reality existed—Corporate America believed it could continue to achieve sustainable rates of return by investing heavily in inventories, manufacturing facilities, personnel, and technology. This, in turn, fueled the need for workers.

We now know that situation was short-lived. Y2K ended up being a bust; those interest rates that were ever so slightly being nudged up in good times as a measure of control had the potential to wreak havoc on the one segment of our economy that was holding its own, housing. Blue-collar employment continued to grow steadily. And then, Corporate America woke up to the smell of overrated expansion.

By now, we have seen our friends and neighbors displaced by unemployment. Today, corporations have 25 percent fewer employees than in the '90s. Our own jobs are in jeopardy. Such phrases as "performance-based compensation," "lateral moves," "contingency employment," "part time," and "temporary" are moving to the forefront of our vocabulary.

The institutions we prized in Corporate America are finding it difficult to sustain phenomenal growth. The balloon is losing air, and there is little anyone can do but hope that economic measures would surface to put the ship back on course. Our government and Federal Reserve did all they could do to alleviate unemployment by putting spendable cash in the hands of Americans, hoping that would refuel the economy. This has been a difficult road to go down.

> ▼ **Today, the corporate citizen must consider his options like never before.**

Today, the corporate citizen must consider his options like never before; companies are retrenching, looking for ways to off-set declining revenues with reduced costs. These measures affect us all. Those bastions that we have long viewed as lasting forever are now toying with our livelihoods; we are not sure how long we will be allowed to play the game in Corporate America. Great institutions are facing staggering losses; companies that had delivered profitable results quarter after quarter are now faced with reducing headcount, shuttering factories, and looking for protection from creditors.

Many strong, viable companies have come roaring down to a sensible reality since the millennium. This reckoning has humbled many companies such as the technology giants Oracle, Cisco, EMC, and Sun Microsystems. They are looking to bring their houses back into order. These are great companies, with great management teams, that will likely recover from this setback. But while companies retool for the future, what happens to the everyday employee who might have invested five, seven, or even ten years to make these firms great? What are employees to do when they feel the microscope bearing down on them and they know the cuts are coming?

This book is designed to address those exact situations. We want you to be better prepared for the coming decade or so of meaningful employment. We're going to look at economic trends, help you evaluate your own employment plan, and make the most of your career. This book was written with the express purpose of allowing the average white-collar corporate employee ages thirty-five to fifty who might be even remotely concerned about his career to be able to recognize those events and circumstances he has control over, as well as those things he does not, and develop a plan that adapts to both.

> ▼ **We want you to be better prepared for the coming decade or so of meaningful employment.**

Success in today's employment environment requires an exceptional understanding of your survival quotient—a combination of internal and external forces at work in your specific career. We are not talking about a new hairdo, embracing a fad diet, or running out to join the same country club your CEO belongs to. You need to consider a best practices approach to analyzing what is happening with your job and what your options are, including the distinct possibility of joining that emerging cottage industry and ultimately understanding the role of "free agent."

Throughout this book, you'll find tips on sharpening your survival skills. And the last section includes a chart you can use to evaluate your own survival quotient. Use this to track your strengths as well as the areas in which you need growth so you can stay competitive in today's tight economic marketplace. Have at it—be honest and be accurate. Remember, once is not enough; do it as often as you think of it. It will help you keep a fresh perspective.

Corporate America has passed the fork in the road. There is no looking back. You might be well-equipped to play the corporate "Survivor" game on your own. But should you need a reality check on where you are, what you are made of, and what you are capable of doing, this book will prove to be useful.

▼

Today's Corporate Climate

As the nature of employment has changed, one concept remains true: Companies have to grow to succeed. We don't have to look too far back to see how this is true.

In the 1980s and 1990s, Corporate America was on fire, with the exception of two short-lived recessions. Shareholder value skyrocketed, and the stock market was out of control. Two things primarily fueled this upward path: revenue growth, and earnings or projected earnings growth.

This growth drove shareholder value through the roof, allowing Corporate America to fatten its bank accounts through public offerings, acquisitions, mergers, divestitures, and the like. This momentum was fueled by individual investors driving up the demand (price) for ownership in these companies. At the same time, the Internet was exploding; start-up companies promised unrealistic projections for growth and profits. The effect was like pouring gasoline on an unattended fire.

Individual investors were literally throwing self-directed retirement dollars hand over fist directly at stocks and mutual funds focused on this "new economy." This newfound money allowed Corporate America and a bunch of start-ups surrounding the Internet to place orders for products and services that they never would be able to consume, in an effort to live up to the dreams they were spinning in the marketplace.

Companies in Corporate America were re-engineering, looking for new economies of scale, which usually led to the deployment of new information systems. These systems were hyped as the cure-all for Corporate America, delivering the dream of new technology to replace the foundation of corporate information. These systems would allow companies to do more with less, allowing Corporate America to thin the ranks of personnel at all organizational levels in the name of growth, thus reversing the trend of secure white-collar employment. These systems also promised trails to new customers and new markets, as well as helping companies stay close to current customers and develop robust, custom one-to-one relationships.

These promises were too good to be true. The claims of these new systems pretty much failed to live up to their promises; yet Corporate America bought them hook, line, and sinker, rushing to replace antiquated information technology. These new information systems cost far more to deploy than originally promised and involved more than re-engineering. They were oversold, delivered late, and failed to meet the expectations of the people using them.

At the same time, the Federal Reserve Bank, the "bank" to our nation's commercial banks, began raising the rate of interest it charged member banks, thus raising the interest rates charged to Corporate America. Chairman Alan Greenspan, a throwback to the Clinton Administration, and his Board of Governors routinely would meet to discuss the financial marketplace and the effect that interest rates might have on our nation's productivity.

Yes, productivity. The Federal Reserve does not just arbitrarily raise and lower rates at the whim of the board; it has elaborate econometric models it uses to estimate actual productivity. The models the Fed was using indicated that productivity (worker output) was continually rising without any effect on inflation. Corporate America believed it could continue to achieve sustainable rates of return by investing heavily in inventories, manufacturing facilities, personnel, and technology.

Fabulous, continued expansion, increased shareholder value—what more could an economy want? In hindsight, it seems that while capital expenditures were high, these models were giving false readings on productivity. The investments in assets, plants, fixtures, and software made by Corporate America were not living up to the promise of increased output. And Greenspan warned individual investors about the stock market bubble.

We now know that this situation was short-lived. The bubble burst and Corporate America woke up to the smell of overrated expansion.

Welcome to the Networked Economy

Today, there is no real security in Corporate America. We must be ready to accept change—frequent, fast-paced change. Many corporations are investing heavily in employee training around corporate change. One of the recent best-selling books is *Who Moved My Cheese?* It takes a very simplistic but positive view of different personality types and how they react to change. Being ready for change is critical.

Often change is surrounded by chaos. Corporate America can easily be compared to a mound of ants. I'm sure we have all wondered how these creatures get anything done; but in the midst of the chaos they seem as though they're on a mission. The life of a corporate citizen often looks like chaos. The term "chaos" was a popular theory in the late '80s and '90s, in which diviners of the day looked to the physical sciences to explain the essential components of the corporate organization. Today, scientists still look for confirmation of minute particles. They know that these particles will never be seen but, with adequate detection resources, they will find evidence that these particles exist. The basic elusive component is called the "quark." Turns out, that fragment that we longed for is described as the basic building block of matter. Unfortunately, this quark cannot exist alone, so why do we continue to investigate this guy? Simple. Understanding the basic components help us to assemble the whole organization.

Let's look at the basic components in the new economy.

No longer does our economy rely on manufacturing. Today, services and service-related industries are king. We've moved from the Industrial Age, through the Information Age, and are now living in the era of the Networked Economy—a world that has been transformed by communication technology.

Communication that used to connect neighbors, friends, family, and business acquaintances has now become the onslaught of global competition. This level of connectivity exists twenty-four by seven by 365. This round-the-clock syndrome is also called the "attention economy": Information is infinite, limited only by the time an individual has in a given day. In this level of access, information is easy to come by, but the ability to take information, deduce knowledge, and control the information is the challenge.

What does the Networked Economy look like and what does it mean for you?

■ This new world places value on ideas, concepts, and innovation rather than what can be dug up, cut down, grown, or simply pushed off an assembly line. The old ways of measuring productivity are gone. Services do not have standardized parts that can easily be counted, measured, and scrutinized. *Your ability to work with information is what matters.*

■ Computer networks enable ad hoc teams to pop up and disappear as needed in a corporation, allowing people to share information and create knowledge. The ad hoc organization suddenly has more value than a structured organizational chart. Team members have to readily adapt to changing needs and requirements instead of adhering to rigid policies and dealing with rules and regulations. *You will need to embrace decentralized authority and decision-making.*

■ Technology allows more employees to work from home. Corporate America is arming its employees with computers that have access to secure corporate networks. That means a company can staff for peak times when customer demand might be high, while maintaining a higher quality of life for its employees—those employees don't have to get dressed, commute to the office, and fight for parking. *These networks not only connect you to other workers; they allow management to keep tabs on what you are doing.*

■ While it is easy to consider the benefits of decentralized workers from a quality of life perspective, be mindful that the water cooler and cubicle city are great places to exchange ideas and stay connected. Recent research indicates that when viewing teams, no one ever seems to work with anyone who is not on his given floor in the same building. There still is value in being able to share our thoughts and ideas on a real-time basis.

If you choose to work remotely, make sure you stay in touch with your internal company network. Visit as often as possible; let everyone know you are coming. If you have the luxury of having expenses covered, make lunch and dinner appointments with your colleagues and, if within company guidelines, pick up the tab.

■ Workers can attach to virtual teams, which are outside the traditional confines of Corporate America. These virtual teams now include fellow employees, business and trading partners, and customers and prospects. These partners might, in fact, be competitors one day and working toward a common goal on another day—it's referred to as "coopetition."

This type of partnering actually evolved from the information technology industry; different vendors and service provider organizations got together to solve specific customers' problems. For example, EDS, which offered services, would partner with IBM for its hardware to propose the sale of a solution to a mutual customer or prospect. These practices are commonplace and, as markets grow faster and faster, companies are forced to cooperate up to and just short of antitrust concerns. Suddenly, your network is of more value than your standalone skills. Managers who are hiring personnel for key roles might be looking at the Rolodex rather than the Rolex: *It's not what you know; it's who you know.*

■ As you mature in your career field, you develop more value. This value hopefully is going to be recognized by your employer in the form of successive increases in compensation beyond normal cost-of-living increases. The '90s saw many corporate citizens jumping from job to job with the effect usually being a nice pay raise. The '90s proved to be a foolish time when many executives in Corporate America overvalued pretty much everything they touched.

This unfortunately has come home to rest with us at the turn of the century. Layoffs, reductions in force, firings, mergers, and bankruptcies have plagued the corporate landscape. The mature employee's value in Corporate America has become suspect and is going to get more scrutiny than ever. The employment marketplace has become more like a swap meet, in which employers are suddenly negotiating for lesser prices on already discounted goods and walking away with functionally competent talent. It's happening in professional sports, health care, education, sales, and all across Corporate America. Some companies are adjusting the way they pay employees. Obviously the best companies in America manage to figure out a way to offer incentives for employees to perform. In the '80s and '90s, it was stock price, stock options, and incentive compensation. *Today, the routine compensation package is the way corporations generate incentives for employees.*

Where the Jobs Are

We've looked at a snapshot of today's corporate landscape. Now let's examine which sectors offer the most corporate success, stability, and survival. Top growth areas for jobs will be:

Permanent part-time employment

Technical health care

Elder care

Biomedical research

Education

Government

Law enforcement

Biometric technology deployment

Counseling

Spiritual/religious leadership

Software development

Information systems integration

Job areas expected to decline:

Full-time permanent jobs

Bricks and mortar retailing

Hospitality

Travel

Aircraft manufacturing

Wholesale distribution

Traditional food service retailing

Service-producing jobs will constitute 75 percent of the job growth during the next decade. Here's a look at some of the numbers according to the U.S. Department of Labor. The categories for growth in new jobs over the next decade are as follows (represented in the order of percentage of growth):

Services	13.7 million jobs
Business	5.1 million jobs
Health services	2.8 million jobs
Social services	1.2 million jobs
Transportation, communications, and utilities	1.3 million jobs
Government	0.5 million jobs
Construction	0.8 million jobs
Agriculture	0.4 million jobs
Manufacturing	0.6 million jobs

Growth Strategies in the New Economy

For companies to succeed, they have to grow consistently, quarter over quarter, year after year. They have to be able to advise financial analysts and the media about their expected growth and then measure up to their promises—promises that have been subjected to the scrutiny of Wall Street.

This growth must be on all fronts—earnings, sales, sales dollar volume per employee, inventory control, improved days outstanding—not just profits. Yeah, yeah, in the late '90s I bought stock in those innovative dot.com companies, which were projecting tremendous earnings in the future. Sure enough, those shares purchased at $70 a share are now worth less than 50 cents. Ultimately, the final measure is continual profitable growth that stays in line with other measures along the way.

To be more profitable, a company can do two things: reduce expenses or increase revenues. Systems deployed in the 1990s to thwart the effects of Y2K had an alternative use. They helped Corporate America bring expenses down, to do more with less— less people, less facilities, less inventories.

The other side of the coin is to grow your revenues in hopes of growing your earnings in parallel. Another hallmark of the Networked Economy is the boom in small companies that are quick to innovate. These companies understand one of the basic tenets of business—innovation, adding a process or product, generates growth.

Innovation often is the only source of growth in companies; they emphasize innovation rather than the wholesale change-out of products and ideas. Look at the impact Southwest Airlines has had on the air travel industry. When other carriers are flirting with bankruptcy, Southwest is defending its low-price model by continuing to reduce the cost per seat mile, and the big carriers are having a difficult time.

The St. Joe Paper Company in the panhandle of Florida owned vast reserves of pulp and timber. It operated a small mill in the panhandle of Florida for more than 70 years, sitting on land that had been purchased at 10 cents on the dollar during the

> ▼ **Innovation often is the only source of growth in companies.**

Depression. Through the years, members of the board, led by family members of the founders, moved away from the highly competitive, low-margined paper business in favor of developing the company's vast land holdings. Today, St. Joe, is engaged in trading, selling, and developing more than half a million acres in one of the remaining pristine resort areas in Florida. St. Joe changed its model completely, innovating in order to grow.

While larger companies have found ways to innovate, the Networked Economy has also seen a boom in smaller, focused firms. Small firms innovate faster, make decisions faster, and can scale up to meet the needs of the customers.

Many larger companies look to smaller companies for innovation. Large mass marketers have made managing the supply chain one of their best competitive threats. This technology wasn't developed in-house; marketers tend to rely on smaller companies to design and build these systems. Suppliers are brought into the manufacturing and distribution process. By keeping these suppliers connected, Wal-Mart and Dell require smaller inventories; in some cases they do not inventory anything until shelves need stocking or computers need assembling.

But there comes a time in the life of a corporation when it has grown to the point it can no longer incubate a new concept or idea due to an overwhelming bureaucracy and red tape. It is unable to successfully develop or exploit new markets or opportunities because of a kind of paralysis that sets in with growth. Then companies have to make decisions about where to invest their capital to yield the best overall return for their shareholders. These decisions often are based not on what the company can make but on what it can buy.

Enter the M&A process—mergers and acquisitions. Mergers and acquisitions are a means by which companies can continue to grow, especially when stock prices are high and bank accounts are teeming with cash. Executives find it much easier to buy their way into a market or product offering rather than take the time to develop it.

Mergers, Acquisitions, Divestitures, and Leveraged Buyouts

The 1990s represented incredible growth with the merger and acquisition trend in Corporate America. Many companies were able to use their high-priced stock as cash and were able to pursue this method of expansion with a frenzy.

There are basically four reasons to do a merger, alliance, or acquisition:

■ A company adds new products or services to its current offering.

■ The company can extend its market presence or geographical reach through the combined efforts.

■ The combined entities gain economies and efficiencies.

■ One company simply overtakes a competitor.

Another popular exercise in Corporate America in the past decade was the divestiture or spin-off. Simply put, a company owns something of value that could be of more value apart from the parent, and the proceeds from the disposition of that subsidiary must be returned to the owners (shareholders) by way of a dividend or payment in kind. The best example might be when you purchase a home that is located on two lots and is positioned so one lot could easily be sold off. The proceeds of the sale are the equivalent of the dividend, and the dividend will be returned to the owner.

Next is the leveraged buyout, which seems to have fallen from favor. I suspect, though, we will see a resurgence, especially in light of the current economic climate.

Eckerd Drug, a Florida-based drugstore chain, is a perfect example of a leveraged buyout done well. Founder Jack Eckerd announced his desire to retire and sell the company he had built. Led by the efforts of the management team, Eckerd employees were able to leverage the company's value in the corporate bond market and meet the terms of the sale with Mr. Eckerd. This was a gutsy move, and the employees were able to control costs while focusing on their core competencies—retailing drugs and sundries. A new suitor, J.C. Penney, came along and expressed an interest in entering the drug store business. Eckerd's owners, its employees, let the company go in a well-meaning salute, and the deal was a win-win for both companies. Since the sale, however, J.C. Penney has been unable to react to market needs and quirks, and the value of the deal has obviously plummeted.

The leveraged buyout is a product of the '80s: "Raiders" disguised as financial clairvoyants set out to take over companies through a series of financial maneuvers.

Financial firms embark on leveraged buyouts using the acquired company's own cash-on-hand, along with corporate "junk" bond financing. Then the new management team breaks up the company and sells off the better assets as a means of raising cash to reduce the burden of debt. The results usually leave parts of once strong companies strewn over the landscape, and a lot of people get hurt in the process.

There are many instances in which companies have almost been seen as poachers, such as Cisco and Tyco International. In the 1990s, both companies used their high stock price like cash, making tax-free transactions for shareholders of smaller entities that they had needed or that had complementary technologies. Cisco managed to snap up some 60 companies during an eighteen-month period, often announcing two acquisitions in a given week. Unfortunately, Cisco's share price fell some 60 percent in 2000 and 2001, and those employees who remained after the acquisitions found that the restricted shares exchanged for the outstanding shares or vested options were either huge paper losses or worst-case tax consequences that they may never be able to overcome.

> **▼ TIP: When your company is going through a merger or acquisition, if you are the acquirer, then you are probably in good shape for the short haul. If you are the "acquiree," your chances of survival diminish rapidly.**

There are also situations in which management teams, employees, and labor unions are able to financially leverage the value of the organization to purchase the company, sometimes referred to as a management buyout.

There appear to be several reasons these newly formed unions fail. One of the biggest reasons is that management tends to ignore revenue requirements and concentrates on cost-cutting measures. Second, management of the combined companies fails to execute on the perceived value of the combined entities. Third, the cultures of the combined entities, mixed with management egos and general lack of concern for the employees, clash, resulting in outright bickering.

Survival Skills for Mergers and Buyouts

Certain types of companies are better suited for mergers and alliances or acquisitions. Statistically, companies in fast-paced industries such as pharmaceuticals and electronics tend to fare better with alliances. More stable, cyclical companies tend to see gains in the merger/acquisition space, such as the recent oil company mergers or the consolidations taking place in the retail banking industry.

If your company is being acquired by a direct competitor, and your industry is thought to be cyclical, the economies of the combined organization might be the driving force in whether you keep your job. It might be time to touch up your résumé. If you are in a fast-paced industry and are in the process of being acquired, your chances of remaining are better. Make sure the acquiring management knows your interests and your skill set. Focus on what you can do for the new entity.

> ▼ **TIP: Weigh your options in a merger, acquisition, or divestiture; this might be a great time to take your profits, and be ready for anything.**

In every acquisition or merger, there seems to be one guy in the acquired company ready to tell the new owners about all the warts and where the skeletons are buried. If you should feel so inclined, *don't do it*! When a management team has put its reputation on the line and shelled out big bucks or used stock for cash to buy something it could not build, it does not want any negativism. Remember what your mother told you, "If you cannot say anything nice, don't say anything at all."

Survival Skills for Divestitures

Many companies find that certain wholly owned subsidiaries or actual operating divisions might perform better if separated from the parent corporation. More companies will be spinning off subsidiaries as a means of realizing the untapped value of assets trapped in the coffers of a parent company.

Usually companies that are spun off do not have access to the best employees of the parent corporation for staffing those areas they have relied on the parent for so long, such as human resources, payroll, accounting, purchasing, brand marketing, and the like. The spin can be of tremendous value to you and has the capacity to raise your "personal stock," that being your own value in the marketplace. This can be a real résumé builder. Your experience of having participated in a divestiture might well be of value to a competitor, as well as other companies contemplating spin-offs.

Spin-offs can have momentum in the marketplace and are likely to need competent personnel to keep the momentum going. If you think you are that guy, stick with it, be positive, do your homework!

Conclusion

Companies, as well as industries, go through cycles and trends. A good example of a cycle might be a Christmas tree grower who cycles through a specific holiday season in a given year, while a good example of a trend might be the information technology explosion/collapse at the turn of the century. These factors, conditions, and constraints affect the posture of your employment future. Be aware of these factors. If you could predict these events, you probably would not need to work—you could spend your days counting your profits from the stock market.

Unfortunately, you need to be prepared for the likelihood of these cyclical events and need to understand the consequences when they happen. Even though you can do nothing about the events, you can be prepared for their effect on your corporate survival.

Survival Tips

■ Be prepared for constant change; make sure you understand the only constant in Corporate America is change.

■ Value in the Networked Economy has shifted from information-gathering to knowledge. Make sure you are well-versed in your company's information stores. Brand yourself as a knowledge warrior if you intend to survive.

■ Expect your corporate existence to become more demanding; the global economy runs twenty-four by seven by 365 and the continental United States spans four time zones. You will have to adapt and be flexible if you plan to succeed in Corporate America.

Questions for Consideration

■ Do I truly understand the impact of the new economy?

■ Am I "buzzword" compliant for the Networked Economy?

■ Am I connected?

■ Am I prepared to change my work habits?

■ Do I have sufficient space at home and am I connected so I could telecommute if requested by employer?

■ Do I understand the implications of the Networked Economy on my industry and my employer?

■ Do I believe my section, division, or work group is viable long term in the Networked Economy?

■ Have I engaged my peers and co-workers to discuss the future of our work unit?

▼

Evaluating the Health of Your Employer

The health of your current employer tends to fall in the category of things out of your control. Sure, you can claim that the sales personnel directly affect the revenue position and the expense of doing business. But by and large, you, as a corporate citizen, have little to no say in how the company does financially. However, it is essential that as a corporate citizen who is dependent on the well-being of the corporation, you keep an eye on things. Especially in light of Enron and WorldCom, who's to know when you could innocently be caught in the cross hairs of a major disaster?

You can be an ostrich and continue along your merry way or you can be an elephant, always upright and never forgetting what you have learned or been exposed to. One of the things that happens in an organization in decline is that the star players bail out quicker than a group of 6-year-olds chasing down the ice cream truck on a hot summer day. Will you be aware of this when it happens, or will you be the one wondering where everybody went?

What can the corporate citizen do when it's not enough to merely stand by and hope all is well? Start with simple things. When was the last time you read your company's annual report cover to cover? When was the last time you investigated or possibly questioned trading activities and partnerships? The recent downturn in the economy has brought many damaging, and potentially illegal, activities to light.

Corporate executives work at the will of the boards of directors representing the owners of these companies, the shareholders. Therefore, those executives are under tremendous pressure to deliver results, meaning improved revenues and higher profits. Basically they must do more with less, quarter over quarter, knowing full well that there is a time when the company will hit the wall.

This manner of accountability is like the trend to rate public schools and the children entrusted to their care. In Florida, there is a test known as the FCAT—Florida Comprehensive Achievement Test. From students' performance on this test, and some other factors, a letter grade is assigned to every school in the state. In order for a school to get an "A" rating, it must be improved from the previous year by a certain measure. At some point, a school does so well there is little room left for improvement and it cannot meet the measure for growth. Corporate America has come to the same point, but biting the bullet and regrouping for another day is out of the question; executives must travel on or run the risk of being replaced.

▼ **Are you an ostrich or an elephant?**

There are two ways to deliver higher earnings and improve the corporate bottom line: grow revenues or reduce expenses. The '90s saw most of Corporate America, under pressure by boards of directors demanding higher share prices, investing in new technology as the newest and best way to deliver better results and improve the bottom line.

This continual pressure caused companies such as Enron and WorldCom to look for creative ways to account for certain relationships and expenses ultimately being judged as a misrepresentation of their companies' financial positions.

Telltale signs usually appear when companies are having problems and a layoff, downsizing, offshore outsourcing, or firing is in order. It's important to be able to recognize those signs, consider all the factors and make wise decisions about your future.

I remember watching the destruction of an institution in aviation history—Eastern Airlines. The perceived problem with

21

Eastern was labor contention. Eastern employees had managed to organize well over the years, and the corporation had trouble managing the collective-bargaining process. The flight attendants, the machinists, the pilots, you name it, all wanted more at a time when industry deregulation and a poor economy said no. As soon as one group finished, another was outside the door threatening a strike that would bring the company to a fast halt. I was headed into Atlanta's Hartsfield Airport after the only remaining solution from Chapter 11 was to dissolve the airline. But the picket lines persisted. Looking at the pilots holding their signs brought to mind the old saying "all dressed up and nowhere to go."

Take a critical look at your employer so you know what to expect about the stability of your job as well as the stability of your company. If you generally do not agree where your company is headed or the direction the management team is leading you and your fellow employees, it is time to consider a new company. Will the company be disappointed to see you leave? There will always be things out of your control and if you feel uneasy, start making plans.

Here are some ways to evaluate your company.

Test the Vision of Your Leadership

Vision is more than a good idea looking for a place to evolve; it's a good idea that has come of age. Apple Computer reinvented Corporate America in the late '70s and early '80s. It thrived on vision—great ideas oozed from every crack in the sidewalk in Cupertino, Calif. Apple made tremendous strides in how it regarded its employees; they became the petri dish in which the newest ideas were hatched and put in motion. Steve Jobs expected his team to think and reinvent continuously. He set the bar high—less than the best was not good enough. Apple was worthy of enacting all that is good in corporate history at its beginning.

But Apple came up short. The company could not separate instilling confidence and making progress. The original founders had the foresight to recognize the value of new products (such as the mouse, the windows-based operating system, the laser printer, and the CD-ROM). But the company failed to see the chaos as a value-added process that would have defined Apple as the strategy to beat, rather than merely a collection of components everyone wanted.

Today, Apple is consigned to specialized solutions in a technology marketplace. Its leadership was not able to sustain the corporate vision. One of the best measures for determining your company's management ability to flesh out a reasonable vision can be the media. Look to what the local press, magazines, trade publications, and financial analysts, as well as your customers and competitors, are saying about your company, its leadership, and the direction they are headed.

> ▼ **TIP: Look to what the media, analysts, your competitors, and your customers are saying about your company.**

Know the Team and the Game Plan

I got what I thought was the opportunity of a lifetime during the dot.com craze of the late '90s. I was asked to head up the sales effort for a relatively new software product that actually worked and had several customers successfully using it. It looked as though it was going to be easy.

What I didn't realize was that the executives failed to have a united strategy for moving the company forward. It seemed as though the top of the organization thrived on incompetence blended with delusions of grandeur; ambush was a prevalent management strategy.

If I had tried to understand the motivation of the management team and the business plan, I would have realized that neither existed. Each executive controlled a specific leg of the business and had his own plans in the absence of a master plan. When we needed to be in the marketplace looking for investment capital, the management team lacked the vision to move forward and spent its time plugging holes. While we were spending money faster than it could be printed, the top managers believed all was well. The market, as we all know, was short-lived and the opportunity to succeed, much less sell or merge, disappeared completely in front of our very eyes. I'm not sure that I could have done anything differently than those managers, but I learned that business plans will tell me whether the management team is in sync or incompetent.

Judge Your Company by the People Who Run It

If you would not enjoy the company of any new executive management team member at your company for a holiday family gathering, start planning your exit strategy. Be wary of letting a guy with a nickname like "Chainsaw" take over the day-to-day management of your company. Shareholders and owners do silly and stupid things.

The power base in your company, division, department, or group is critical to the company's overall well-being. Join the group; it can be beneficial to your long-term well-being. But make sure that, in the process, you retain your identity. Selling your soul to the devil for a short-term gain is foolhardy.

Where are the Lifeboats and Who is Going to Do the Paddling?

Watch for the telltale changes in management in your company. Shortly after the acquisition of a company, I saw the new guard begin a slow, continuous reorganization. The new hires and the newly acquired, who were in favor of change, were in constant conflict with the old guard, who worshipped the culture of the parent company. Yet the company had grown stagnant. It needed to enhance the product line while looking for new ways to sell it. Diviners posing as highly prized business consultants ascertained that the company needed to get to know the customer better; thus, the process of change began.

New levels of management emerged, filling holes and chanting the mantra about cautious transformation. During this transformation process, the company was reorganized several times, finally forming a new structure. The organizing managers of these new structures chose to treat their respective structures as kingdoms. These gurus started bringing in their own people, whether the new subjects of the kingdom had any likeness to the old company or not. These new leaders just kept paddling that lifeboat, and their loyal subjects from previous encounters just kept jumping in.

This is a time of great caution for a company man. We all know of many instances in which well-meaning employees' careers have been pushed aside in favor of a newly emerging power base—new management. New managers will bring in their own loyal workers, and those connections can melt your years of service the way kryptonite impairs Superman's ability to leap tall buildings. Don't expect new managers to be loyal to you because of your years of service to the company. Generate new loyalty by buying in to their goals and objectives. Make sure you are in sync with the management team and that you understand their goals and objectives.

> ▼ **TIP: Your key asset in the new economy is your intellectual capital.**

Be an effective team player—you need to be on the top of your game. Proper deployment of assets is critical to the survival of the company, the team, and your career. Your intellectual capital is the sum total of what you know. Learn to convert what you know into knowledge. Then use that knowledge to your advantage. Those caught doing so are often rewarded beyond their dreams.

Measuring Success

Financial and industry analysts consider many factors when they determine the overall health of a company, but, at the end of the day, shareholder value is everything. As long as the share price is going up, then the natives (the shareholders) are not restless. Executives keep their jobs by making the shareholders wealthier; after all, they are the owners.

You should become familiar with other metrics, such as: sales growth, quarter over quarter, year over year; EBITA (earnings before interest, taxes and allowances); sales dollar volume per employee; and return on net assets employed. After all, there is a good chance that these metrics are used to determine how the executive management team of your company is compensated, and we know what rolls down hill.

Public companies produce lots of reports that are available to the public. Here are some you can use to evaluate your own company's health.*

■ 10K and 10Q Filings

Public companies are required to make available routine filings containing quarterly and annual financial results, disclaimers, market changes, and future plans, as well as expectations of future results for their companies. These filings contain commentaries about the market conditions, competition, industry sector, and likely pitfalls of the company. These reports can be found at the EDGAR website of the Securities and Exchange Commission, www.sec.gov. The EDGAR site contains a significant portion of the company's historical filings, allowing you to compare numbers for yourself.

Reviewing your company's 10K (annual) and 10Q (quarterly) filings will allow you the unbridled opportunity to test your own thoughts and concerns about your employer. Expect there to be numerous mentions toward worst-case scenarios, but also you can read between the lines about the company's thoughts regarding mergers, alliances, and acquisitions.

Continued earnings (profits) at the same time as a declining

---

* In Corporate America, there are several types of businesses, including the publicly traded corporation, the foreign-held American Deposit Receipts (ADR) corporation, the privately held corporation, the partnership, the sole proprietor, and the not-for-profit corporation. The public corporation and the not-for-profit corporation are the only ones generally required to publish financial information. For purposes of this book, we will be looking primarily at public corporations and the requirements for reporting on their financial health. The business principles, however, generally apply to all businesses.

cash flow can suggest a specific weakness—be on the lookout. Also, if the company is taking a significant write-down (or one-time charge), it likely has taken money from the bottom line to shore up a big mistake. These tactics are becoming commonplace in light of the foolish antics some companies played in the '90s buying anything that got in its way. Make sure you understand why these companies are taking these write-downs.

The rules about these filings are getting stricter, and companies and their external auditors are feeling significant pressure to fess up to the concerns for the company rather than overlook the trivial matters. Take the time to read and understand these documents; it does not cost you anything, and your job might depend on it.

■ Annual Reports

Every public company is required to produce an annual report. These reports must discuss all disputes and lawsuits under way, patent infringements, failed government approvals, and missteps in the marketplace. They also must include an audited accounting of the company's financial performance. The SEC and IRS, as well as other state and federal agencies, require this accounting to adhere to GAAP (generally accepted accounting practices). Usually an audit firm would attest to the findings and claims made in the report.

> ▼ **The handwriting might very well be on the wall; just look for it.**

In the 1990s, many high-tech companies made claims of outrageous projections for their wares and services. Those exaggerated claims hurt not only unsuspecting investors but also employees who left other good-paying jobs for the promise of significant gains in the stock of their new employer. Scrutinize unwarranted claims of phenomenal growth and understand that those public auditors, hired to scour the books of the company and substantiate the unheralded claims, are under contract to the company, not you the employee or shareholder.

Management and the board of directors are ultimately

responsible for what is published in the annual report, but they have a vested interest in seeing that the best spin is on the ball. You need to read these reports with critical eyes and understand their implications for your job and position. The handwriting might very well be on the wall; just look for it.

Who Says?

Some companies come forward and offer guidance about their expected financial performance. Others refuse comment. If your company makes statements, be sure to follow the news releases, subscribe to an Internet service delivering financial information, follow the news, and mentally chart the company's performance over time. The management of publicly traded companies will, from time to time, meet with industry and financial analysts, often staging elaborate events around announcements and new product rollouts.

Find out which analysts track your company's stock and keep abreast of their comments about industry conditions, buy/sell ratings, and the like. These analysts could belong to a world-renowned financial brokerage firm that trades in your company's stock, or they may represent an industry association or an independent firm specializing in watching specific industries. Find out who these people are. They are respected as having knowledge about your company, the management team running your company, the marketplace they operate in, and the competitors in the market.

Watch for these statements, specifically watch for warnings coming from your management team regarding lowered revenue and earnings estimates as well as loss of significant contracts, customers, or the departure of certain longtime management team members.

Looking at the Books

Companies hire accounting firms to audit the books for the benefit of investors. Public companies must produce a reasonable accounting for the past year's activities in the company. Generally an accounting firm certifies that the findings of a given quarter or year's accounting are on the up-and-up according to GAAP (generally accepted accounting practices).

The audit firm tries to strike a delicate balance between the billable hours associated with representing a client and its reputation for doing the right thing versus what the client wants attested to. A change in audit firms usually points to a difference in opinion between your company and the audit firm. For example, the audit firm may want to recognize a specific point, statement, or collection of points, and the management team disagrees.

> ▼ **TIP: Subscribe to a financial newswatch service. The Internet has many to offer, and many are free. If you have an online relationship with a discount broker, the brokerage is likely to offer the service at little charge, delivering news about your company, and its customers and partners via e-mail.**

If you were found to merely suggest that these conflicts even existed in the late '80s or early '90s, you would certainly have been subject to ridicule or, worse yet, laughed out of a room. It was a gentlemen's thing, you know, like talking about your second cousin (the one who was doing hard time for some misdeed) over the Thanksgiving turkey. The late '90s, however, proved this was a legitimate problem. Marvels of mathematics were standard operating procedures for some companies, as seen with Arthur Andersen and its statements regarding the health and well-being at Sunbeam and Enron.

The first telltale sign of accounting trouble is when a company must restate earnings or fess up to a new set of numbers. When a management team deems it necessary to revisit past revenue claims, cold shivers go down the spines of any board of directors. The board's actions are supposed to represent the best interests of the shareholders; it can be a culpable offense if the board has misrepresented the facts.

> ▼ **TIP: Keep track of market and financial analysts who track your company, industry, or marketplace. They can be very insightful about your company, its products, its competitors, and the like.**

It is hard to tell whether your company or its auditors are juggling the books, and it usually does not come to light until after the fact. Read all the reports and understand what is going on. Also watch the chat boards on the Internet regarding your company or parent company. Well-meaning, disguised whistle blowers often will tip their hand on the Internet.

Recently, questions have been raised about analysts keeping comments and ratings high for certain firms in exchange for certain highly profitable business contracts. But expect to see this cleaned up quickly.

Insider Holdings

Who are the big shareholders, how much do they own, and are they selling? If the suits in the corner offices are selling, you ought to be selling, dusting off your résumé, or at least asking why. Today, it is harder for executives to dump large blocks of stock, especially with the media watching. Watch trading activities about your company; they can offer clues about the direction your company is headed.

Make sure you know who is dumping stock and why. For example, Steve Raymund, chairman and CEO of Tech Data, the second largest information technology distributor, sold a large quantity of stock in his own company. When asked why, he said he was balancing his portfolio. That's a reasonable explanation. Most executives have a tendency to be over-weighted in their own company's stock. This is a bad situation for any investor, whether a high-flying corporate executive or a middle manager with years of service to a given company.

> ▼ **TIP: Never invest more than 10 percent of your worth in your company.**

Look at the poor employees of Enron. They were forced to hold company stock invested in their retirements while insider executives were trading large blocks of the stock. Keep your portfolio balanced, so you won't be hit too hard by any single holding.

Customer Reaction

What are your customers saying? Are the once-full parking lots at retail stores empty or have the phones stopped ringing? Are your products and services meeting the needs of your customers or are they over-priced or antiquated? Are you confident that your company's offering is hitting the spot? It is always easy to find someone in-house to tell you how great a product is or how much better things will be in the future. It's harder to look for those telltale signs of lost momentum or declining demand.

Conclusion

It's up to you to understand the many variables of the equation that determine the health of your employer. Learn from the debacles of Enron, WorldCom, and Tyco. Take off the rose-colored glasses and take a critical look at your company. Understand the effects of your management team's vision. Know the value in being a team player. More importantly, evaluate whether you actually have a permanent position on the roster. There's plenty of information available about the financial health of your employer. Find it, read it, and use it to the benefit of your career.

Then find out what others are saying about your employer. These are the tools you can put to work for your career.

Survival Tips

■ Understand the overall vision of your company.

■ Be aware of the value add your company brings to the marketplace.

■ Know who is at the helm of your company, the members of the management team, the board of directors, and such. Know where they came from and what other boards they possibly sit on.

Questions for Consideration

■ Are you an ostrich or an elephant? When was the last time you attempted to second-guess your company, its management, its vision, or the direction it was headed?

■ Do you really understand how your company makes money?

■ Are you plugged in to the leadership of your work unit?

■ When was the last time you read an annual report cover to cover (including the fine print)?

■ Do you know where to find the other published documents about your company?

■ Do you know which financial and industry analysts follow your company?

■ Do you know who really owns your company?

■ Do you know who controls your company and where they derive their power to do so?

Section Three

▼

Evaluating Your Corporate Value

A dear friend of mine had a stellar 23-year career in sales. His product technology had been getting long in the tooth, and his competitors were making strong inroads in a market he was used to dominating. Every day he was able to draw on his every skill, do a significant gut check, muster all his capability, and continue to win time and time again. But each win got harder. It seemed the tide was going out and never planned on returning.

My friend failed to spend time gathering information on opportunities. He did not take the time to self-assess, but tended to react based on gut feelings. This lack of planning and lack of short-term and long-term goals left him holding the bag. Ultimately, he succumbed to the pressure; he threw in the towel and joined a fanatical new competitor. During the gut-check process, he would have been well-advised to look at his temperament, but he did not have the guidance of knowledgeable friends and peers. These were uncharted waters; the digital world was here and he was not ready for the change.

Job security has disappeared in today's economy. We see Corporate America shoring up its ranks through downsizing, rightsizing, restructuring, alignments, divestitures, reductions in force, and the like. As a typical corporate citizen you are likely to face a termination sometime in your career. That means you can't expect a company to look out for you. Job security is what you make of it. Your future rests with the value you bring to the company you serve.

You should always keep in mind the value of what you do. Even better, be flexible and prepared to increase your value. In this chapter we'll look at ways to evaluate and increase your value to your employer. Live it, believe it, then be a part of it. Better yet, to quote Jean-Luc Picard of *Star Trek: The Next Generation* fame, "Make it so!"

Know Your Customer

Acquiring and keeping customers in today's economy is everything. It is important that you understand who your customer is. It might be a Fortune 100 Corporation or it might be an internal department or group in your own company. The Networked Economy is so bold as to suggest that the day of the mass market has passed, and you should segment your customers to oblivion. That means you need to know your customer so the parts can be assembled to meet his needs. Your knowledge about your customer, whether internal or external, is crucial to your success. This knowledge suddenly becomes your value add in this new economy. Creating value cannot be done effectively unless you know your customer.

Be an Innovator

Constant innovation is vital for healthy economies; the '90s were evidence of that with the advances made in biomedicine, pharmaceuticals, and information technology. Look for places other than the obvious for innovation. Often, that nagging problem that keeps you awake at night is that next opportunity for innovation. Take ownership of problems; get next to them. Today's problem could be tomorrow's innovation.

At the time the U.S. government deregulated telecommunications, allowing for long-distance competition, AT&T had little competition. MCI was poised to make a big change in how business was done. It was not designing a new way to communicate over long distances but saw ways to innovate in how we acquire it. MCI, with its determination, hard work, and planning, invested in attracting commercial users with a direct sales force.

You have to think of yourself as an MCI; you have to come up with better ideas, ways to improve processes, generate better revenues, or reduce costs for your customers.

Make sure your best ideas and innovations are credited to you. Companies in decline tend to have their ranks filled with hangers-on, people desperate for a good idea.

> **▼ TIP: The best way to be talked about is to innovate and be productive.**

Fight for Your Customers

Today's "frictionless" marketplace makes change easy—not just in business but in most of our society. When was the last time you called the cable company, long-distance provider, or a cellular telephone service suggesting a better deal was available from a competitor? Your current provider is usually quick to match the competitor's offer but will ask for something in exchange, such as signing a year's contract: It wants you to have some skin in the game. As individuals, we negotiate every day; but we often fail to realize it.

It's the same way in Corporate America. It's easy for a customer to leave your company for another. Companies fight for customers every day. The company in first place can always expect to have competitors nipping at its heels for that number one spot. It will forever be fighting to remain at the top. The competitors always are looking for deals to lure the customer away. They may offer a free trial, saying that they'll pay the cost to switch back if a customer isn't happy. (In reality, the switch back can be a very time-consuming process. Yes, your old company is happy to have you back, but getting reimbursed for any cut over expenses can be traumatic.)

This movement of customers is called "churn." And the ability to switch or have your customer base churned has been exacerbated by deregulation. The airlines did it to promote competition, the telecom industry did it, and now the power companies are in the midst of deregulation. The opening of telecommunication markets through deregulation is actually the primary cause for the Networked Economy we are living in today. This allowed companies to have greater flexibility, and they embraced this notion of frictionless commerce.

Always keep in sight of your customer; there is always someone out there ready to take them from you, even internally in Corporate America.

> ▼ **TIP: Have an action plan in place to keep your customers, and keep it current.**

Embrace Change

A great deal of emphasis is placed on time in the new economy. I'm not suggesting that you wear several wristwatches in an attempt to keep up with your customers, partners, team members, and prospects around the globe. But you need to pay attention to cycle time, the amount of time it takes you to get a product or idea to market. Markets for new products and services are forming overnight. Be ready to fill those markets.

In the '90s, Corporate America needed to replace or update aged accounting systems. I saw firsthand how these systems got justified and watched boards of directors approve replacing these systems before the fallout of Y2K. I also saw the anxiety incurred by organizations just attempting to make these new systems work.

The biggest problems were the "whiners," employees who chronically complained about the new way of doing things. These systems were justified, based on the threat of Y2K and the sheer fact that the company would be able to do more with less.

When Corporate America was cutting—to do more with less—there was no room for any "whiners" after these systems were deployed. Those whiners topped the list when the RIFs and layoffs happened.

Take the Right Chances

When you have the occasion to seize on a new opportunity, think carefully before engaging. If the opportunity happens to be one created by someone else or one that has been in existence for a while, take caution. The phrase "perception is reality" should ring loud and clear. If this good fortune, in fact, was deemed a success at the time of hand off, it is likely to be a monumental undertaking to actually receive credit for any accomplishment. A great supporting actress in a movie is important, but it's the one at the top of the marquee who gets top billing, always.

> ▼ **TIP: When you have a new process or method being imposed by management, embrace it. Do not be a "nay sayer."**

At one point I was handed a floundering customer relationship. It was one of the luckiest things that ever happened in my career. The customer had significant potential, but the person who did the hard work—getting everyone to agree to everything—didn't get the time necessary to see the fruits of his labor.

Needless to say, I did see the fruits and to this day I am ever thankful for his efforts. I spent two years making a name for myself almost at someone else's expense, but that's not the whole story. My efforts during that two years catapulted my career like nothing else; I was able to parlay my success into the career move of a lifetime.

Obviously, the move required I hand off the golden goose to an individual who was certainly more creative, harder working, and better suited to fit the needs of the opportunity. He spent the next couple of years trying to prove to everyone that he was responsible for the success of the account. My hat is off to both of those individuals.

When starting anything—a new job, assignment, or project—start at the bottom and leave on top. This is what people will remember about you.

Do not be guilty of being recognized as having been given

something or, conversely, as the person who will run a good thing into the ground.

Keep Learning

Gone are the days when you would get a degree and then join the workforce. Education is now a lifelong process. Corporate America needs skilled workers to compete in the global economy, and workers need to keep their skills current to be able to compete for jobs. This shift from the information economy to a knowledge-based economy will be the true test of the value of any corporate employee.

In Arizona during an education conference, a speaker launched an Internet search based on the word "California." It resulted in more than 20 million hits—stores of data in which "California" was mentioned. He said one would need an "electronic shovel" to get through this vast amount of data. Search engines such as Google allow you to limit the confines of the search by eliminating certain categories. In this demonstration the speaker went on to segment the search criteria, getting to 100,000 sites—still too many to comprehend but worthy of examination. Yet all the speaker wanted was the average annual rainfall for California. Know the question first, before you engage. Master the art of divining the correct answer. Make it look easy.

Employees who can master the new knowledge age will be the big winners. The "knowledge worker" is simply someone who gets paid to think. Whether you believe it or not, you are quickly becoming a knowledge worker. And greater knowledge leads to higher salaries, new positions, and increased responsibility.

Companies continually look at how they can utilize knowledge as an asset. Information and knowledge are intangible assets; you cannot really point to and hold knowledge. But the individual who can formulate information into knowledge becomes a tangible asset. Many software programs store information about such topics as products, services, and customers, but your ability to react to the information makes you unique and an asset to your company. Because there is so much information available today, make sure you know what you are looking for. Understand the question or deficiency at hand and formulate a plan to gain the knowledge or skill necessary to answer the question or correct the problem.

Evaluate Your Skills

How well have you developed your skills to ensure you are an asset to your company? When you improve your skills, you increase your overall performance and your value to the organization.

■ Using the SCANS Inventory

In 1990, the secretary of labor's Commission on Achieving Necessary Skills (SCANS) assembled labor, education, and business leaders to define skills that are required for high-skill, high-wage jobs. SCANS identified concerns that employers had about the ability of employees to perform basic analysis and communication functions.

Below are the five basic SCANS competencies: resources, information, interpersonal, systems, and technology.

● *Resources*—Developing resource skills means students can allocate time, money, material, and human resources. Examples: creating timelines, preparing budgets, or writing a job description.

● *Information*—Gathering and evaluating data, either from existing sources or by developing new ones; organizing and maintaining information; interpretation and dissemination of information; and computer proficiency. Examples: implementing a record-keeping system to store information, making oral presentations using multimedia devices, or literacy in software programs such as PowerPoint, Microsoft Excel, and Microsoft Word.

● *Interpersonal*—The ability to be a team player, teach others, provide good customer service, demonstrate leadership, negotiation skills, and sensitivity to cultural diversity. Examples: work with a team to solve a problem, train a peer on the job, handle complaints both in person and on the phone, the ability to delegate, or show an understanding of people of different cultural and ethnic backgrounds and how they need to work together.

● *Systems*—Understand how technological, social, or organizational systems work and the ability to function within them. Examples: create or interpret organizational charts and understand how all parts of an organization work together to create a product.

● *Technology*—The ability to solve problems through the use of machinery, computers, or other technologies; as well as the ability to distinguish between computer programs, deciding which ones will produce the desired result. Examples: read technical specifications, set up or build equipment from instructions, troubleshooting, and keeping equipment in working condition.

> ▼ **TIP: Create an inventory of all the skills, both basic and advanced, that you have attained.**

Create an inventory of all the skills, both basic and advanced, that you have attained. Then review that skills inventory often, identifying the skills that need to be updated—especially in areas such as technology, which tends to change every eighteen months.

The SCANS inventory can help you evaluate your strengths and identify areas for growth. It is also a valuable tool when you are evaluating a career change. You can perform a gap analysis between the skills required for the new career and your existing skills. The results can be used to design a skills development plan.

■ **Using a Performance Evaluation (The 360 Process)**

Many corporations use performance evaluations to track the achievement of their employees as well as determine deficiencies. Many public companies make a conscientious effort to establish formalized evaluation methods. These often involve carefully packaged, sanitized processes from outside firms specializing in employee evaluation assessment. Performance evaluations usually are mandatory for every employee in the organization. The result is the corporation's written record of an employee's service, attitude, and loyalty toward the company. This history, combined with "at will" laws in a given state, is usually a pretty good beginning in protection from unwanted employment lawsuits.

As an employee, the evaluation gives you the opportunity to compare your skills and performance with the company's expectations of your position. This is your chance to see where you are in sync and where you fall short.

One popular form of performance evaluation is the 360 process. Collectively, you, your peers, your subordinates, your customers, and your managers, as well as human resources professionals, gather the data to document your performance. Over time, these efforts generally portray an adequate representation of your employment history at the company. You will find the 360 evaluation process as a good means of measuring areas of competency. It also measures competency upstream and downstream, as well as among team members.

> ▼ **TIP: The evaluation gives you the opportunity to compare your skills and performance with the company's expectations.**

Most performance evaluations today include a series of surveys that conform to standard measures, set against a predetermined set of goals and objectives. The manager/human resources professional will document facts pertaining to the current appraisal. You will normally have an opportunity to examine and/or contribute to the document prior to any permanent recording. These documents can be the basis for an increase in compensation, so make sure the process is fair and thorough. Worst case, these documents also become the basis for selecting low performers in the event a reduction in force becomes necessary. That's why it's called "rank and yank." Companies rely on performance reviews when it's time for a "corporate cleansing" as a means of making room for new blood.

Use the performance review to see what skills your employer is seeking. And remember that this is a permanent document. Examine it carefully. If you suspect that comments might have the opportunity to be contrived or taken out of context in the future, voice your objection and, possibly, you will be allowed to recommend adequate wording of the record.

Going Back to School

To perform in the Networked Economy, all of us will need to develop new knowledge and skills, sometimes on a real-time basis. Instantaneous knowledge is available today via the Internet; it is called "Just-in-Time education." We're not necessarily talking about a well-rounded education but the need for knowledge about a specific subject or matter. People can get answers to their questions as soon as they ask them. The Networked Economy allows you to sift through the mounds of information to gain the knowledge needed at that time.

You can find this JIT education process either on a formal or informal basis. Formally it is known as distance education; informally it is called surfing. Just-in-Time education means constantly upgrading your skills and knowledge base, often supplementing or replacing what you might already know.

It might also be necessary to acquire new skills through more conventional methods. Many times employees are eligible for tuition reimbursement when these sessions are applicable to the job being done for your company. Companies that offer tuition reimbursement for classes that pertain to your job will often have a stipulation making you responsible for a portion of the tuition should you resign within a certain amount of time after completing the coursework.

There are many avenues for gaining additional skills or certifications. Many recent college graduates have some sort of a technical certification like MCSE (Microsoft Certified Service Engineer) or a CNE (Certified Novell Engineer). Many colleges, universities, and other private institutions offer courses and training to attain these certifications. A current trend today is the

Executive Certificate of Completion, learning certifications, or degrees through distance learning.

Collaborative Learning

For years the learning process was considered to be largely an individual activity, something that ended with personal achievement and success.

Today, Corporate America often looks at learning as a team effort—parts of the organization learn in a concerted effort, either jointly or individually. This concept of Corporate Learning is nothing new. In 1970 a company called Lotus Notes began the design of a collaborative software product that allowed groups of workers to join together to achieve a means. This collaborative effort through software became known as "groupware."

> ▼ **TIP: Know the areas in which you need additional training, and find out how to get it.**

In fact, the software industry as a whole has been built on similar collaborative efforts. There are instances in which development teams based in the United States would work on software from daylight to dark, only to package up the day's efforts and beam them by satellite to other countries, where complementary teams would either debug the day's efforts by the U.S. teams or continue the development effort. This can only be possible with modern-day development tools that allow for the checkout, annotation, and documentation of software in which many people have been engaged around the globe.

Collaborative corporate learning begins to form a community of practice in your department, division, or company. Work becomes distributed among the members who offer the most experience or time to complete task. This effort begins to build a bond inside the group, a social cohesion that converts information into usable knowledge that ultimately leads to competitive advantage. In order for a company to stay on its game, it must make the most of knowledge at the employee level. That means it needs to engage in research activities, allowing employees to collaborate and creating teams to experiment and test new theories, as well as investing in new ideas through acquisition of smaller, more nimble firms. The employees of these knowledge-driven firms will set the pace for innovation inside the company as well as in their respective industries.

> ▼ **TIP: If your company is knowledge driven, be recognized as an innovator or implementer. If your company has not employed a knowledge management strategy, get involved; this is your opportunity to be recognized as a visionary.**

This view of knowledge is only just finding a foothold in mainstream Corporate America. If your company embraces these efforts, volunteer to join a collaborative team; if it doesn't, see what you can do to encourage your section, department, or division to begin the process. Bringing in an outside facilitator to jump-start and monitor the process is not very costly. And management will notice your efforts, which very possibly could be the foundation for your next assignment or may very well be a skill that your next employer will covet.

Conclusion

The Networked Economy represents a significant opportunity to excel. There are many innovations that allow you to develop value with your employer and add value to your career.

The economy has quickly shifted from a culture in which information reigned supreme to one in which knowledge is crucial. Corporate America has the information necessary to engage its employees in a knowledge-based marketplace. It is time to innovate; use the creative juices you have to outshine your co-workers.

Understand who your customers are, both inside and outside the company. Knowledge allows you to understand what it will take to keep those customers happy, thus keeping you in demand.

Change is imperative; it's on every street corner. You have to embrace it to survive, no matter how discouraged you get or how difficult the task.

And you have to embrace learning on a real-time basis; learn to use the tools available and enhance your marketable skills through outside learning methods. Not only grasping but also engaging knowledge in the Networked Economy can be the deciding factor in surviving or withering away.

> **▼ TIP: Being recognized is imperative in this Networked Economy. Make sure you are being talked about and not just on awards day.**

Once you have ascertained the value of increasing your skills in the workplace, you need to keep a running tab of them. Create an inventory of those things that will be of value to your present employer but also that might be of value to a competitor or even a prospective employer in a different industry. Often we do not know our own value until we shop it around.

Survival Tips

■ Know your customers, both internal and external.

■ Be known as an innovator by your co-workers, peers, supervisors, and management.

■ Be ready to embrace change at the drop of a hat.

■ Understand that learning is a lifelong process.

■ Keep a running tab of your certifications, skills, talents, and acknowledgments.

Questions for Consideration

- When was the last time you had to fight to keep a customer?
- Are you versed in your company's tuition reimbursement policy?
- Do you know the five basic SCANS competencies?
- When was your last 360 performance evaluation?
- How did you rank overall in the company on your most recent evaluation?
- How did you rank within your department, unit, or work group on your most recent evaluation?
- Do you have a list of possible skills that would enhance your career? Were these skills identified in your most recent evaluation?

Section Four

▼

Creating a Lifelong Career Plan

So we've gotten through our evaluation of our current employer as well as taken a good look at the value we bring our employer. Now the information must be converted to action steps. It's time to put a plan in place and stick to it.

Good planning can lead to a rewarding and satisfying career—or two. If your long-term and short-term career development plans are carefully orchestrated, you will be able to maximize your potential in the workforce today and in the future.

Career development really involves understanding yourself and your potential, and then aligning this with the personal goals you laid out to achieve lifelong happiness. Meaningful planning includes your lifestyle, surroundings, and environment, as well as the ones you care for the most—your family unit.

There is no single formula that defines the path to personal success. Every person has a different concept of success. We all have different goals and priorities. We have strengths and weaknesses that are part of our inner workings. Personal inspection and inventory is one way of helping us arrive at our own personal goal of success.

Not only does each of us have our own vision of success, we often can find ourselves living up to someone else's idea of achievement. We can lose sight of what is truly important to us. If we spend our time and effort trying to meet somebody else's idea of success, and ignore our own beliefs, we will find ourselves unfulfilled and miserable. We must recognize that other people's values are no less important than our own, but we can find ourselves miserable if we focus solely on other people's values and do not seek work that is more in line with our own.

Career planning is not a one-time event but rather a lifelong effort in which factors continually change. What is your personality type? What are your skills? Do you have sufficient education and training? What are your interests? What are your goals? What do you want to accomplish in life? The answers to some of these questions may stay the same throughout your career; but, chances are, many of these answers may change.

> ▼ **Career planning is not a one-time event but rather a lifelong effort.**

As we look at our careers, we need to look at the long-term and short-term aspects of planning. Short-term career planning is tactical. Those things that are done in our day-to-day employment situation tend to be short term. Long-term planning, on the other hand, tends to be strategic.

Forward-looking planning might involve a series of several short-term maneuvers that will form the basis for a long-term strategy. Let's say you consider taking a lower-paying job or you are willing to relocate as a means of positioning yourself for a longer-term, better paying position, which might help you advance in the company or result in increased compensation. This tactical short-term maneuver would be the basis for a longer-term strategy. This longer-term strategy then becomes part of your lifelong career plan.

Early in my career, I remember moving to be nearer a key customer and the management office responsible for my well-being for the short-term impact. I left the security of a performing sales territory in favor of a longer-term career opportunity in management. I was able to position myself for career advancement by doing this, thus facilitating a longer-term goal. While both of these strategies involved relocation, one enhanced my present situation while the other had further-reaching opportunities that would have a lasting impact on my career.

Make sure your long-term career planning takes into account

lifelong learning as well as the flexibility to change job functions, employers, or even careers. Let's face it; with declining population growth in the United States and the results of Sept. 11, we will have fewer foreign nationals to supplement our workforce. You will most likely be working past retirement age.

Personality

Understanding our own personality type can be the basis for defining, setting, and accomplishing our goals. As we understand our own strengths and weaknesses, we can improve our personal skills.

The quicker we become aware that we live in a world where certain qualities and traits are more suited toward particular tasks, the sooner we are on the road to success. At one point in my career I worked with an individual who found out that he did not have the personality type to function in a sales environment. It was unfortunate. He had spent his entire college experience preparing for a career in sales when he might have been better suited as an accountant or information technology professional.

Should you find yourself described as a "type A" personality or aggressive, you might be well-served dealing with people, face to face, possibly in a sales or spiritual role. On the other hand, should you find yourself described as analytical, you might be well-served as an engineer or architect. If you long for the outdoors or love to work with your hands, you might be quite comfortable in the construction business. Whatever you and others think about your personality type is probably true.

Here are several questions to ask yourself (it will help if you write down your answers):

- What is important to me?
- What are my dominant traits?
- What are my supporting traits?
- Are these traits balanced?
- How do I grow, knowing all this?

When you have taken the time to assess your interests, strengths, and likes, then apply them to selecting a career, you most likely will not have to endure the stress of working in a field that you do not enjoy or waste time and money on training for a poorly chosen career.

Most of us have a tendency to overexpress a particular trait, leaving us deficient in other areas. This tendency to favor the dominant trait (thereby hindering other traits) is common but tends to keep us from developing those secondary and tertiary traits properly and can lead to an imbalance in our personality type.

We see this extremist tendency in our perception of those personalities who conquered the Silicon Valley. They include names like Steve Jobs, Gordon Moore, and Scott McNealy. These pioneers and their subordinates tended to stick to their dominant tendency at the expense of all other traits. Left unchecked, a tendency to favor one dominant trait often can obscure your other traits. This type of dominance is not common and may be the result of years of conditioning.

Therefore, we must use the understanding we acquire from our self-examination to strengthen those weaknesses rather than to excuse any poor behavior. Companies often look for well-rounded people for advancement. The well-rounded individual is deemed to be able to deal with other subordinate employees. Make sure that in dealing with your imbalances you are certain of your own ideas and that you are not listening to the ideas of co-workers. In any instance, we cannot be responsible for other people's behavior, but we can control our own and that is what will get us where we need to go to fulfill our needs and desires.

From time to time we are stressed to the point of serious imbalance. But if you frequently experience these issues, seek professional help. Counseling and medications can easily bring balance back to your life and help keep your career on track. Investigate your employer's benefits program. Many employee assistance programs exist that will, with a simple phone call, put you in touch with a health care or mental health professional. Don't let mental health issues or issues of alcohol or substance abuse derail your career.

Looking inward helps us understand the significance of our

style in our personal growth. It also gives us the opportunity to better understand those around us. Suddenly we become aware that a specific personality style might be more conducive than another in a given situation.

Not only do we understand ourselves better, but also we can see how personality strengths and weaknesses affect other people's behavior. These insights are extremely useful and powerful. We see why people react certain ways in certain situations. Each personality type has strengths and weaknesses. That helps us work together better and helps us realign our expectations of others.

During my career, I had the opportunity to work for an individual for whom I have considerable respect. He proved to be a valuable mentor and afforded me my initial experience in management. Many people in the office considered him aloof, or even stuck up, most likely due to his British upbringing and conservative nature, but our partnership worked well. He proved to be a great sounding board and

> **▼ TIP:**
> **Companies often look for well-rounded people for advancement.**

mentor, and his tactical, analytical style complemented my strategic style.

People come from every walk of life, different religious beliefs, backgrounds, educational levels, and sexual orientations. Individuality begins to play an importance in how we interact with individuals and groups of individuals. We realize quickly that we will not completely understand why these individuals think the way they do nor will they understand our way of life, but possibly, we can reach these people as a means of making this a better world in which to live. The individual who takes the time to consider another person's point of view finds it easier to function in the world of Corporate America.

Individual assessment can have many uses. It can assist us in the area of personal growth and measuring achievement. Learning to apply certain behaviors can be a powerful tool.

Understanding one's personality type and being able to appreciate the personality types of others can quickly accelerate one's career.

You won't be able to create an effective and realistic career plan without taking a good, hard look at your own strengths and weaknesses.

Looking Ahead

Let's also look at some trends and predictions for the next few years that will help you chart your course. The future is wide open. As workers, we need to look at these trends and begin to assess how they will affect our future careers. We will be forced to accept change, in the workplace, in our lives, in our careers, and in how we think about the future.

■ **Expect Changes in the Population**

The population of the United States is the determining factor on the size of our workforce in America. In the next decade, the workforce will grow from 141 million to 158 million men and women over age 16, according the Department of Labor. At the

> ▼ **TIP: Watch the trends, and question how these changes will affect your job outlook.**

same time, the workforce will become more diverse. White and non-Hispanic segments will fall from 73.1 percent of the total workforce to 69.5 percent. By 2010, Hispanics will constitute a larger portion of the workforce than blacks. The growth of women in the workplace will outplace men by about 4 percent.

By 2010 the youth labor force (ages 16 to 24) will expand to nearly 17 percent of all workers in the United States. Workers ages 25 to 54 will make up nearly 67 percent of the workforce, down from 71 percent in 2000. Workers age 55 and older will constitute the remaining 16 percent of all workers. Expect changes in the population. Watch the trends, and question how these changes will affect your job outlook.

Appendix One addresses the laws that protect the growing

segment of our corporate workforce that crosses the 40-year-old line.

■ Older Workers

The present employment situation for baby boomers, estimated at 88 million people, can be called bleak. There are some 25 million to 38 million baby boomer employees in Corporate America. While in late 2001 and 2002, we saw massive job loss in this segment of the population, it was no worse than in any other segment. But the baby boomers feel the pinch in a different way because they have complex commitments.

As employment growth overall slows, older workers might find a bit of reprieve. During tough times, older workers tend to be less likely to lose their jobs. But once they're out, it is more difficult for them to be re-employed, according to the General Accounting Office.

> ▼ **TIP: During tough times, older workers tend to be less likely to lose their jobs.**

So, will older workers be able to find meaningful employment? There is a labor shortage on the horizon, and older workers can find solace in it. In 2001, the first baby boomers turned 55 years of age. In 2015, 20 percent of all workers will be 55 or older according to the Bureau of Labor Statistics. The number of workers who are following the boomer generation is much smaller. The labor force growth, while presently at 1.1 percent annually, will slow to 0.7 percent annually by 2025. The Bureau of Labor Statistics says this will create incredible demand for the graying workforce.

In addition, most employers are not considering the implications of the graying of America's workforce. For example, according to surveys published in *Government Technology* magazine, half of the employees in state government nationwide will be eligible for retirement during the next five years. Education is facing a similar crisis; nearly half of all educators have 20 or more years' experience. Federal, state, and local governments are dependent on these older workers. They contain the institutional memory that government has not been able to capture about various processes, systems designs, and legacy applications. Government fears the day it will have to replace large blocks of employees who carry significant knowledge that affects the delivery of services or the collection of data and revenue.

Employers in both the public and private sectors will be under additional pressure to find suitable, experienced workers when the economy improves. The pressure will first be felt in the public sector. Those employers have frozen hiring and salaries. When companies start looking for additional workers, they will be looking at those beyond the traditional retirement age.

> ▼ **TIP: There is a labor shortage on the horizon, and older workers can find solace in it.**

On one hand, private and public employers see the benefits of younger employees. Older workers are not as desirable or as productive as motivated younger employees. After all, older workers are perceived to be resistant to the type of changes necessary for survival, and the cost to train them is excessive compared with younger workers. When we hear Corporate America speak about older workers, they offer glowing praise but fail to actually add to the ranks when faced with openings.

But let's look at the benefits of an older workforce. Older workers today are healthier, smarter, and more willing than ever before. Once they are trained in the new ways of the world, they tend to be more prompt, incur fewer lost hours of work, and their overall impact on benefit programs is less, considering their child-bearing years have passed. Older workers generally are more adaptable to peak and seasonable demands for more output and servicing of customer and management demands.

Most employees of Corporate America interviewed for this book do not intend to fully retire; they plan to find working arrangements that offer them the security of income while allowing for work arrangements including part-time employment and seasonal availability. This all leads to significant pressure on the U.S. Department of Labor to amend the rules governing pension regulations so older workers can stay in the workforce, resulting in the need for new legislation that encourages incentives that would allow employers to keep older workers.

■ Keeping Up Appearances

There never really is a good time to bring up the telltale signs of aging, but this is as good a spot as any. There are obvious indicators about age, such as changes in hair color, hairline, weight, wardrobe, health, and overall attitude.

> ▼ **TIP: When companies start looking for additional workers, they will be looking at those beyond the traditional retirement age.**

I have seen several companies use the "culture" as a means of describing the impact of age as it pertains to success in the organization. The appendix of this book outlines laws governing discrimination. This section will deal solely with the things that will improve your perception in the workplace.

I am no slave to fashion myself; especially as I get older, I have gotten comfortable with my habits and style. And by no means am I qualified to offer fashion tips, practice medicine, or play amateur psychologist. However, it is important to be cognizant of your appearance in the workplace.

Recently, I contacted a good friend, whom I had not seen in years, about getting together when I was planning on being in the same city where he lived. Before the call was over, I got a very uncomfortable feeling from the other end of the line, almost as though my good friend was trying to tell me something. Well, that something was that he had colored his hair. I certainly had no intention of letting on to anyone in the office; as a matter of fact, when I had the chance to make a private comment, I did, sincerely complimenting the gutsy move.

Right after leaving college, a good friend and I visited a mutual friend for a weekend in Daytona Beach. Quickly, we were introduced to his group of new friends. Having grown up together and having played every seasonal sport together, we had a habit of using one other's last names rather than the first (which is still a tough habit for me to break when I get to know someone). It seems that this mutual friend had significantly changed the pronunciation of his last name. Boy, were we surprised when we heard someone call him by this new pronunciation! We did everything to keep from letting on about our surprise and settled for just "Dave" that weekend.

> ▼ **TIP: Make sure you are not dating yourself by your appearance or attitude.**

Make sure you are not dating yourself by your appearance or attitude. This can often cloud the perception of co-workers or management. It may very well be subconscious, but it can happen. If you have tended to put on weight as you age, make sure you adapt your wardrobe.

If you have difficulty hearing, make sure you see a licensed audiologist. There is nothing more annoying for young people than to have to slow down or repeat themselves. Listening technology has improved tenfold over the past decade. If you need help, get it.

Any additional comments about appearance would be out of place here. Suffice it to say, pay attention to the details when it comes to how you might be physically judged.

■ Aging Population's Effect on Society

In two decades, one-fifth of the population in the United States will be over age 65, and 46 percent will be over age 50. Combined with increasing life expectancy, zero population growth, and improvements in health care (such as advances in bio-medicine and genetic engineering), an aging population will have dramatic effects on social services and society at large. Strategies in the public and private sectors will need to be devised to care for the aging population. And we can expect shifts in public funding from education to accomplish this task.

■ **Social Security payments will increase by 35 percent over the next two decades.**

Even though the government says it will never happen, just do the math. In 2013, Social Security will pay out more than it takes in. With so many people reaching retirement age, the only way to keep Social Security afloat is to raise the employer/employee contribution and the retirement age.

Do not be totally dependent on Social Security for your retirement. There will be something in the pot, but how much depends on the changes made to the system. My advice is to make employer-based retirement contributions if you want the quality of life you have likely become accustomed to in your working years.

■ **Thirty-five percent of all workers employed full-time will work remote.**

The events of Sept. 11, 2001 have taken their toll on workers. Employees have fresh concerns about their safety and they have seriously re-assessed their priorities. Corporate America has been in transition during the past decade in an attempt to geographically disperse workers, having sales personnel and sales management located around the country or globe. More and more sales professionals are working from their residences. Corporate America has been able to reduce the cost of maintaining offices to house personnel associated with sales and marketing activities. And companies have devised specific strategies for these organizations to have access to information systems and data about the customers they service, deploying Virtual Private Networks (VPN) and gateway-access strategies. This trend will continue. Your next job could well depend on the availability to work remote; having an office in your home will be of great value in your career.

■ **The ASP marketplace will be revived.**

In the next decade, as much as 80 percent of all new corporate information systems will be outsourced, and the large infrastructure companies will be ready, reinventing the ASP (Application Solution Provider) marketplace. The ASP hosting model in technology is not new; it was the rave in the late '90s with the dot.com boom. This time, expect to see the regional Bell operating companies, their subsidiaries, the large long-distance providers and companies such as AOL-Time Warner to be ready to fill this void.

The dot.com/ASP marketplace will re-emerge, offering Corporate America the systems it needs for the future, completely integrated and web accessible. It will eventually live up to the claims of the '90s. There will be a quantum shift that will occur, revitalizing the telecom providers as they connect and integrate these extended enterprise. This extended enterprise will become the most valued resource of the corporation, in which your information can be turned into knowledge.

■ **Education as we know it will shift from a graduation/degree-based system to a certification system.**

The K-12 education systems will be further taxed with the lack of funding as well as responsibility of training our youth for careers. Another paradigm has shifted here. Last century, we saw a system in which students were expected to get their education then join the workforce. The new educational systems will shift from this "learn it, then put it to work" system to a system of lifelong learning. Certifications for certain skills can easily become more valuable than the actual degree. Often today in the field of medical technology and computer networking, we see well-meaning people who have left highly specialized fields to pursue careers in these fields.

We will begin to see the educational system pointing students toward careers much earlier. Students will be able to select paths that result in their being fully certified for a specific job upon completion of high school. In fact, many students today pursue vocational training in lieu of more traditional college preparatory programs. The certification system that is emerging is, in fact, the apprenticeship of our past.

We can expect to see less reliance on traditional ivy-covered education in favor of needed training and placement. We can expect to see less self-directed education to enhance one's credentials, but more emphasis of predetermined courses of study as a means of continuing education. Many professionals who continue to remain engaged in the self-control of their trade are requiring this process to maintain the skills necessary to perform the task associated with the job market. The legal, medical, education, and trades fields are requiring this level of education to con-

> ▼ **TIP: Certifications for certain skills will become more valuable than the actual degree.**

tinue in their fields. This requirement for licensing often requires proof of completion of certain courseware needed for an individual to be licensed to continue to perform a certain job.

These changes, while appearing to be new, are actually a return to our past, much like those days before we knew jobs as we do today.

■ **Commercial travel will consolidate over the remaining decade.**

Since Sept. 11, 2001, we have seen the devastation imposed on the travel industry. Business travelers are reluctant to just hop on an airplane to visit customers or attend meetings and conferences. Airlines have ceased operations, filed for bankruptcy, laid off employees, and taken federally guaranteed loans to continue operations. Other airlines, such as Southwest and Jet Blue, have prospered, not by doing a better job but rather by innovating. Other reasons for the success at Southwest include using only one type of aircraft, reducing services to the traveler by limiting advanced seat selection, and making more stops and reducing time at the gates rather than adopting the expensive hub system for connecting travelers. This innovation helps make their airfares competitive, resulting in a profitable revenue management model for all airlines.

Lodging will continue to see a decline in overnight travelers and the individuals or real estate investment trusts who own most of the hotels and lodging in the United States will begin to suffer. Most of the financing of these facilities is done through mutual funds and corporations. Although real estate has proven to be an excellent alternative to the stock market for investment, that bubble can also burst. Mom-and-pop establishments will begin to buckle because of fewer travelers and the implications of the costs associated with the Americans with Disabilities Act for equal access.

As a point of reference, these buildings could be adapted to house our elder population. The Marriott Corporation has identified elder care as a significant opportunity and is investing as such in adult managed care as well as vacation interval ownership.

The food service, restaurant, and rental car businesses associated with commercial travel will continue to feel the pinch of a stagnant economy. Car rental agencies will begin by selling off their fleets and reducing purchases for the manufacturers. These agencies are often franchises owned by independent entrepreneurs who are going to be caught in the cross hairs of higher costs and lower revenues.

■ **The dependence on the dwindling and foreign supply of oil will cause prices to rise to $50 per barrel.**

The terrorist acts of 2001 and the continued violence in the Middle East will be enough to limit the supply of oil. The increased demand will force prices higher until we reach a point that safer drilling and remote locations such as Siberia and the North Slope will be offset by the higher cost. The war on terrorism will continue to see sanctions against countries such as Iraq, Iran, Syria, Libya, Sudan, and very possibly our good friends in Saudi Arabia. The governments of these countries are unstable; we have seen the impact of religious extremism in Iran and Algeria since the fall of the shah of Iran as well as the antics of Colonel Kadafi. The leaders of Saudi Arabia, who have been close friends to the United States, are actually a loosely held faction representing the tribes linked through a king and his family. Someday, these governments will likely disintegrate in favor of a handful of religious leaders who will favor more conservative ways. These events will surely lead to less available oil for the United States, whether out of reduced production or absolute disdain for the American way of life.

Russia, which maintains one of the most abundant as well as remote sources of energy, will continue to suffer from corruption to the point that, economically, the only thing it can do is allow for the exploitation of the country's natural resources: oil, coal, and timber. The move toward capitalism has not been without its faults. Russian commerce has developed in the same pattern as the Industrial Revolution in the United States, resulting in the price that is paid to maintain civil rest. The uncertainty of availability of the Russian supply of oil will certainly play its role in significantly driving up the price of oil.

■ **China over the next two decades will surpass Japan, Germany, and Great Britain and become the second-most prosperous nation in the world.**

It is time to do some math. At the turn of the century, the average monthly income in China approached $94 per person while the United States' average monthly income was $2,739 per person. In Japan the number was $2,646 per person, and in Germany, $2,454.

During the past 20 years, China has become the sixth-largest economy in the world. China's average annual income per person has risen an average of 10 percent per year per person in the past decade, and the average income per month probably will continue to grow at 7 percent annually, yielding some $300 per month per person by the end of the next decade. The population of China is likely to be nearly 2.5 billion people in 2020. The sheer numbers created by multiplying the population by the average annual wage will outweigh every other country.

China has two resources worth considering: cheap labor and a burgeoning middle class. India, Pakistan, and Taiwan all have appeal in the labor market but have a stagnant middle class, quickly finding itself overpriced for the market of skilled and semi-skilled workers. The sheer power of the numbers is enough to push China ahead of many other countries.

■ **The European Union (EU) will bloom over the next decade.**

The merging of the countries of Europe will continue as a means of expanding the global economy and banding together to correct the ills of our past. While we have seen struggles on a cultural basis as well as monetary, the result will show that this is the only way countries can compete in the global economy. Expect to see similar strategies deployed in the Pacific Rim as well as in North America, with the United States banding together with Canada and Mexico for improved trade, security, and mobility. The concept of a single world economy could likely happen in our lifetime.

■ **The entertainment industry as we know it will undergo significant business process re-engineering.**

Content in the form of information and entertainment is already changing significantly. The music and software industries have struggled with piracy. But Napster was on to a new way of doing business; it was an industry innovation—innovation that the music industry failed to come to grips with. Napster has come and gone, but consumers' habits for acquiring music have not changed, nor will they. The music industry will just need to begin working through the issues rather than fighting over them. To quote Bob Dylan, "The times they are a changing."

The rest of the entertainment industry will follow suit, whether it's better delivery of pay-per-view or unlimited access to movie libraries. There will be a revolution, preceded by innovation. Conventional methods of distribution will not be adequate.

Quality time in an individual's life will be more important than ever as we spend more time at home. Access will be important and markets larger than we ever imagined will be the delimiter of the future. Life as we know it will continue to change at a very rapid pace.

■ **Legislation regarding genetic information will increase, pitting state and federal governments against the insurance industry.**

The availability of so much information is almost overwhelming. What can we possibly do with all this data? One thing is to assimilate it to into knowledge. But one of the biggest threats associated with all this data is that it could deny an individual his their rights. Current legislation protects the privacy of citizens' medical data. HIPAA (the Health Insurance Portability and Accountability Act) is phase one of a much longer process. Imagine that you find yourself being denied certain medical insurance coverage because your provider has access to genetic information as well as your medical history.

> ▼ **TIP: Science will be turning all the information associated with the mapping of the human genome into knowledge.**

In the next decade, science will be turning all the information associated with the mapping of the human genome into knowledge—knowledge that is intended to help mankind, possibly extending our lives and retarding the aging process. On the other hand, that same knowledge can as easily be used to interpret your genetic makeup, allowing certain underwriters to speculate about your vulnerability to certain illnesses and conditions. They could ultimately deny you specific coverage for certain types of costly coverage or treatment. This is scary stuff; we cannot let this knowledge that is being contrived for the better of man be turned against us.

■ **Your medical records will be your personal property.**

Today, your health records are your personal property; you have the right to request your health record from your physician. The information in your records is valuable to insurance companies, drug companies, and employers. HIPAA (the Health Insurance Portability and Accountability Act) represents a challenge to every health care organization. Few organizations have the staff to devote to keeping up with and understanding the laws, implementing remediation measures as needed, and tracking changes in the standards.

Your medical records will become safer than they ever have. The information that can be passed among insurers, employers, and providers will become more restricted. This level of privacy will definitely confound our health system. Employers will be required to keep an arm's-length distance between benefits claimed and employment records. Violations are likely to be over-looked while the health system, providers, and employers only begin to understand these issues.

It is believed that this confounding of processes and data will eventually lead to a national health insurance program. Every person in the United States deserves access to adequate health care. The costs of avoiding this decision are likened to the tobacco legislation our country has experienced. In a similar way, the cost of not having a national health insurance program outweighs the cost of having one.

■ **Biometric technologies will become present in every walk of life.**

The biometric revolution is quickly becoming a mainstay of the economy in America. The acts of terror associated with Sept. 11, 2001 will press this technology into play quicker and faster than we ever imagined. Biometric technologies already play a growing role in our society. A simple visit to Disney World in Orlando is likely to result in a finger scan for re-entry or use of a single ticket that will span more than one day. Airline passengers in London approach iris-scanning kiosks during the ticketing process. Visitors to a trendy nightlife section of Tampa, Florida, are subject to facial scans, which law enforcement personnel use to compare with images of suspected criminals.

> ▼ **TIP: Beware of the rise of identity theft as our society's reliance on biometrics increases.**

So banks have begun to deploy biometrics associated with transaction-based systems such as credit and debit card identification. This technology will quickly be incorporated to protect valuable information inside Corporate America, legal documents, or medical data—especially when remote access is important. Biometrics will be used in the future to strengthen identification documents such as driver's licenses and passports. State governments have been collecting digital images of drivers for several years. Soon they will be digitally storing these images with other pertinent documents such as birth certificates, visas, immigration forms, and parole documents.

Beware of the rise of identity theft as our society's reliance on biometrics increases. Some twenty digital driver's license systems have been stolen from offices across the state of Florida. The false identity marketplace is big.

Look for biometric technology to be quickly added to the identification process, whether using a debit card to make a purchase at the local grocery store or applying for your next job.

■ **Real estate prices will decline by 15 percent through the decade as the demand for suburban homes declines.**

There is expected to be a significant migration from our major metropolitan areas by middle-class America to smaller cities and towns. Access to the virtual workplace will contribute significantly to employees wanting a simpler lifestyle that cannot be afforded in large cities. The demand for suburban housing will decline, resulting in lost values of properties. Estimates in the greater Northeast are for declines of 20 percent to 30 percent, while the growth states such as Florida, California, and Washington will be considerably less. These declines are relative certainly juxtaposed to the fast-growing real estate market following the economic downturn of 2001. We can expect fewer people moving because of job-related activities.

In the past three decades, we saw people moving on an average of every five years. Employees of large corporations often moved every three years for the sake of job advancement. Today, the need to move has subsided with better transportation, improved communications, and the need to be nearer to your customer base. Many people are finding it easier to remain in one location and manage the effects of job changes while keeping families in the same location.

Watch for this trend to take hold as people look at their priorities differently and technology allows their jobs to be done from virtually anywhere. After all, work is everywhere, there is plenty of work to be found, and it's the jobs that will change.

■ **States, counties, and municipalities will be faced with significant overhauls of tax and zoning regulations.**

The effects of a faltering economy and the events of Sept. 11, 2001 are wreaking havoc on our tax code. Here's how the tax code, generally speaking, is categorized. Currently, our federal government tends to rely on taxing income and dividends of citizens, imposing excise taxes on fuels and communication services as well as the distribution of wealth associated with inheritance. States, on the other hand, typically tax the sale of goods, collect excise taxes on fuels and communication services, collect fees for services, and tax incomes of residents. Cities and counties rely on municipal sales taxes on goods purchased, income taxes on residents, and ad valorum taxes on homes and properties.

An overhaul of our tax code will occur later in this decade. Today, states are looking at new methods of taxation. Some are adding a sales tax on services, medications, and food, while others are investing heavily in technology to build data stores that can be examined on an ad hoc basis to determine those areas that warrant a second look. States are comparing income with taxes paid for individuals over periods of time. When the income tends to increase and the taxes paid decline, red flags appear and lend credence to investigate the claims made by the taxpayer.

I think we will see a swap of the tax models of the federal government and the states. The federal government will move to a sales tax model of collecting taxes, while states will become more reliant on individual and corporate income taxes, and cities and counties will continue to tax as they always have. This represents a monumental shift in the tax code and will be heavily debated in statehouses and Congress for years to come, but this is necessary given our current state of affairs.

Conclusion

There is a phenomenal shift occurring in our midst. The population in the United States is expected to grow by more than 24 million people in the next decade, according to the U.S. Department of Labor. Continued growth obviously indicates the need for more consumer goods, creating the need for workers in manufacturing and distribution. While growth is good for the expansion of our economy, it will affect certain occupations differently than others. The population growth in certain geographical areas and ethnic groups will seriously affect future employment trends.

The Hispanic population is blossoming in the United States, and the Chinese (and for that matter most of Southeast Asia) are increasing their standard of living daily. This will affect our futures. These groups of people will quickly become the largest users of the goods and services we are employed to deliver. Make it a point to better understand their needs, learn their customs, and become proficient with their languages.

> ▼ **TIP: Consider the changes in the population and their effect on your career plan and long-term goals.**

At the same time, portions of the U.S. population will move from one segment to another through the natural course of aging. The 55- to 64-year-old age group will increase by 11 million people in the next decade. An older population defines the needs for different goods and services. We are witnessing one of the greatest transfers of wealth in history as the parents of baby boomers die. These baby boomers are aging as well, and emerging groups are coming to prominence. Consider the changes in the population and their effect on your career plan and long-term goals.

The way we do business will change. Prior to Sept. 11, we usually conducted business in buildings surrounded by other buildings. It was done face to face. The tragedy of 9/11 has left an indelible mark on how we will do business. Security will be at a premium. Not only will our information need protecting, but so will our offices, workplaces, homes, churches, and places of commerce, as well as our way of life. We should become accustomed to less face-to-face interaction. We can expect to be working from our homes in the future, placing us closer to our loved ones. We will have to make sure we are up-to-speed on the latest communications and information technology systems in the marketplace. It is time to brush up on our skills at operating in a decentralized fashion. We have grown far too dependent on a centralized way of life; we now have to be ready for change, be ready to embrace the decentralized way of doing things.

Expect the institutions of our past to change. Governments will become engaged in our lives. Health care will be more proactive and much more pervasive. We will be living in a more localized environment while working in a global marketplace. The things that we have placed significant value on in our past will change: Tangible assets like buildings, plants and inventory will shrink in significance; knowledge will be the key. Intellectual property and the ability to innovate will reign supreme over anything else we can do in the marketplace. We will need better ways to handle the information stored in file cabinets and computers as well as in people's heads. The knowledge we derive from this information must be protected from our employers, other people, and companies that stand to gain from access to the information. Make sure you can craft knowledge from information; this will be the key to your future.

Be aware of the trends that will affect the development of your lifelong career plan. We have to pay attention to these factors if we expect to stay ahead of the game. Sure this section could have easily dealt with résumé writing and interviewing skills. If that is what you think you need, then I suggest hitting the closest bookstore; you will find thousands of titles on the subject. This book deals with factors that will affect you in the future, such as the availability of oil, minority population growth, the effects of aging on the workforce, as well as the major trends this author sees affecting how we live and work in the future. Believe it or not, you are likely to have eight job changes in your useful work life and possibly change careers one to two times. If you are lucky enough to have the luxury of 30 years and a gold watch, consider yourself privileged, because most of the readers of this book are likely to work well past retirement age, whether by choice or necessity.

Survival Tips

■ Know the strengths and weaknesses of your personality type. This will help you in dealing with other people as well as make you a better team player.

■ Understand your own goals, objectives, wants, and desires. Make every effort to live up to your own expectations, not those of someone else.

■ The workforce will age; adapt your expectations to that trend. Try to contemplate the impact of an older workforce on your career.

■ Expect to see a significant overhaul in our tax system by the end of the decade.

■ The Big Five Personality Test is a great source for a personality sanity test (www.outofservice.com/bigfive).

Questions for Consideration

■ Are you prepared to work remote from a home office?

■ Are you prepared to work permanent part-time, allowing your employer to staff up for peak demand?

■ Are your ready for the possibility of having to hold a part-time job to make ends meet?

■ Do you speak a second language?

■ Are you prepared for a real estate bubble much like the one experienced in the technology sector at the turn of the century?

▼

Engage the Right Investment Adviser at the Right Time

One of the key tenets to corporate survival is laying the groundwork for long-term financial stability—your retirement—and being prepared for any situation in the short term, whether it's an opportunity, a disability, or an unexpected loss of job. It's vital that you be prepared for any circumstance life throws at you. A solid financial foundation and a thorough understanding of benefits in transition are essential for navigating a successful professional career. Without these fundamentals, you limit your opportunities and you may jeopardize the financial security of your family.

Don't risk your financial stability by going it alone, or even relying on the advice of family and friends. Successfully navigating these important issues requires the help of a professional investment adviser. You want a licensed and trained professional who will understand your goals, look after your interests, and work to ensure your financial security. This is not a decision to be taken lightly. The future of your family is at stake. You need someone you can trust.

There are a lot of well-informed people parading around as self-appointed investment advisers in this day and time. It is important to seek the advice of a professional when looking to secure your future as well at that of your family. There are a lot of different investment advisers ready to help you, with a wide array of acronyms after their names that look like alphabet soup: Certified Financial Planner (CFP), Chartered Financial Analyst

(CFA), Chartered Financial Consultant (ChFC), Certified Public Account/Personal Financial Specialist (CPA/PFS), Chartered Investment Counselor (CIS), Chartered Life Underwriter (CLU), Certified Fund Specialist (CFS), Master of Science in Financial Services (MSFS). These professionals are well-trained and their survival is usually based on the sale of products that they represent or their company represents.

There are three broad classes of investment vehicles—insurance, legal, and financial—and each has its own purpose. You need to understand the differences among them, know when it is appropriate to engage with each one, and know from whom to seek this professional advice. Be leery of the many part-time people using investments and insurance as a second occupation. It does not cost you any more to seek the help and advice of a professional.

Financial professionals or, rather, investment advisers, generally come in one of three

> ▼ **TIP: To avoid serious financial setbacks, find counsel in a trained professional.**

flavors: a broker, a financial planner, or an insurance agent. Consider forming relationships with all three: trading stocks, bonds, and mutual funds with your broker; establishing long-term vehicles such as wills and trusts through your financial planner; and engaging the services of a professional insurance agent to mitigate your risk and gauge the needs of your family in the event you are unable to work or you die.

Funny thing, though. When you approach the three classifications of financial planners, you usually will get different answers from each to that age-old question: Where do I begin? The insurance agent is likely to recommend cash-value life insurance. The broker might suggest switching (trading) around your holdings to better fit your current investment picture. And the financial planner might suggest investigating the use of a trust to minimize taxes at your death. All three are correct to some degree. Do not try to engage all three at one time; seek the counsel of each one independently. After your future is fully in play, you may consider getting two or all three of these individuals in a room together.

Getting Started

No matter where you begin, just do it. You will need all of the following:

■ A brokerage account for your Individual Retirement Accounts or 401(k) rollover.

■ A will, a living will, and a durable power of attorney to make sure your final wishes and instructions are carried out the way you want.

■ Plenty of inexpensive disability and term life insurance to replace your salary in the event you are unable to work or you die. This can easily be obtained through your employer. If not, see your insurance professional.

Because the financial decisions you make have long-term consequences, you need reliable, competent professionals who are working for you, not for their own bottom line. How do you find qualified help and evaluate whether they are the right fit for you?

Look for the professionals who take the time to understand your goals—about short-term success as well as retirement needs—and listen to their advice. A licensed professional will likely abide by your goals, weighing the risks of investments to match your needs. Look for that trained professional.

■ **Seven Tips for Selecting an Investment Adviser**

● Be prepared to discuss your existing financial situation, goals, and risk profile.

● Get recommendations from friends, relatives, and other professional advisers—accountants and lawyers.

● Conduct personal interviews to make sure you feel comfortable with the adviser. He is going to be helping you make some of the most important decisions in your life. Make sure the adviser asks a lot of questions before he starts drafting a plan or selling any financial products. He must completely understand your current situation and goals.

● Question the adviser on training and certifications.

● Check the background of an adviser to ensure there are no disciplinary actions.

● Understand how the adviser is compensated. Know whether he is motivated to sell a particular investment instrument.

● Ask how you fit into the adviser's clientele. You want to be represented by someone who has similar clients and can give you appropriate attention.

There are two basic types of professional licenses that investment advisers carry—a Series 6 and Series 7. A Series 6 license generally is for professionals selling life insurance. Series 7 is for selling mutual funds, stocks, and bonds. Make sure you understand the type of license your professional carries and know whether he is eligible to sell the security you are interested in purchasing. If he does not hold the license but someone in his office does, then meet the individual holding the license. Better yet, go by the office, make sure it is local and then ask a lot of questions. Look at the furnishings and specifically look at the awards posted in the lobby or in your professional's office. Make sure his name is on the award(s) and that it is not some certificate of completion or team award for a great sales quarter. Seeing your professional's name means one of two things: either he is doing a great job servicing his customers or he's a great sales person. Most likely he is both.

The investment adviser's job begins by consulting with you and your spouse or significant other to understand your finances and financial goals. The adviser will help you identify problem areas and draft a financial plan based on goals, attitude toward risk, and desired return on investments.

The use of these professionals will cost you a good deal; their knowledge does not come cheap. And the cost of the transactions they handle is determined in one of several ways. In the most prevalent method, commissions are paid up front, decrementing the invested balance. In another popular method, the investment is offered as a no-load (no-commission) investment. Here, you might receive a lower rate of return for a period of time or be subject to a penalty for early withdrawal. Never be afraid to ask for a lower price or better commission scheme. Investigate alternative payment options other than the traditional commission plan often incurred when using brokers and insurance agents.

In the past, stock brokers have been guilty of pushing clients to trade stocks, equities, and holdings frequently, or they might spread a client's account across several mutual funds, unnecessarily creating lots of small buckets instead of a few adequate buckets. In either case, they have maximized their commission at the client's expense. You will find that, no matter whether you are using a loaded or no-load fund, the more you buy from one fund or family of funds, the more likely the cost is less. And insurance agents have, from time to time, focused solely on the financial instruments their representing company was pushing, usually offering a higher commission. Often, insurance professionals will take your need for a retirement strategy and put it in a fancy wrapper such as an annuity or whole-life policy. Neither is bad, but make sure you know what you are getting and what the alternatives are. Remember, do not leave all your investments up to one individual, only to find they all are with insurance vehicles or are in the stock market. Distribute your investments among the three classes. Spread it out.

> ▼ **TIP: Never be afraid to ask for a lower price or better commission scheme.**

Investment advisers, and many brokerage houses for that matter, now offer to manage a client's portfolio for an annual fee, usually of 1 percent or so. You pay a percentage of your assets in exchange for advice and usage. So if your asset value goes down, they get less; if it goes up, they get more. Your adviser no longer has the incentive to make unnecessary changes or, as the industry likes to say, churn your account. Keep in mind that managed accounts generally have dollar-limit thresholds, meaning you have to have a $50,000 minimum invested.

When you talk to an investment adviser, you might want to bait him a bit with certain questions to find out where his heart really is at: Is it your future or is it his pocket book? You might suggest that you are contemplating cashing in your company stock or possibly exercising accrued stock options to pay off your mortgage. The gains from the sale of stock or the exercise of the options represent a sizable commission opportunity for your adviser. So hear him out; watch the body language. If you are not satisfied with the initial reaction or suggestion of a strategy, you might want to find a new adviser.

Also, if you employ a full-service broker, make sure you have a corresponding discount brokerage account, just in case you decide to move some dollars around or need to relocate a 401(k) account. The discount brokerage account will cost you far less in the long run than a full-service broker. You can be on your own.

Financial Primer

In the last 40 years, we've seen an order of magnitude's growth in the number of methods to save and invest your money. IRAs, SEPs, 401(k)s, and other investment vehicles offer a dazzling, and sometimes baffling, variety of ways to bolster your retirement funds. And in times of job transition, COBRA and other federal statutes have been put in place to protect you.

The purpose of this book is not to cover all the aspects of the financial marketplace, but rather to offer a primer of financial decisions and benefits that are part of employment. You need to understand the benefits and limitations of these options and work with your investment adviser to put together the best package for your individual needs and the long-term security of your family.

Retirement Planning

Gone are the good old days when folks spent their entire career with a corporation and, in return, retired with a sizable pension. In today's economy, professionals change jobs too often to accrue many pension benefits. And the dynamics of pension funds have changed dramatically. So today's professional can't count on the corporation to provide a significant pension. It's up to you to manage your own retirement planning using a complex set of options provided by various employers, as well as setting up retirement plans that are independent of any corporation.

Educate yourself, attend seminars, read the financial section of the paper, and never get intimidated because you do not understand. Stop the company's benefits representative or your investment adviser in process and ask him to re-explain the information until you fully understand the concepts, rules, provisions, and costs. It's your job to understand the vehicle in which you are investing.

Financial Markets

Retirement planning is one of the most agonizing events you will ever endure. When you think you've got it licked, something changes. The bear market in 2000 left many people ill-prepared for the decline in value of their retirement accounts. They suffered tremendous losses in stocks that had outrageous values imposed by a marketplace willing to run up the price of any entity with a dot or a com in its name. Many people were hurt because they expected returns of 12 to 20 percent when, in reality, the value of their portfolios was over-rated by 40 to 90 percent. To add insult to injury, many of those investments will never recover.

The agonizing effects of 2000 should be cause for all to take warning. Seek the advice of the licensed professional and stay the course; watch out for barroom advice about ditching retirements in favor of new after-tax schemes. Be wary of sure-fire tips from well-meaning friends and acquaintances. One of the best tips for retirement planning is: *Don't react emotionally to the events of Wall Street.*

Here's my experience. I was always intimidated about financial markets. I had a good idea about how much I was worth on paper but had a difficult time discussing the various financial instruments I had working for me. I decided to overcome that deficiency and embarked on the ride of a lifetime that did nothing but line the pockets of brokers and hucksters. The $50,000 I spent with these folks gave me the education of a lifetime. I could have spent a lot less on textbooks or seminars and learned financial lessons. But the real lesson was the one I learned from the brokers. The losses incurred in trading options and investing stocks will never be duplicated.

When I finished with that foray into the financial world, I was buzzword compliant to the point that, at most cocktail parties, friends avoided me because the topic of conversation usually evolved around that day's personal trading experience. I finally realized the ills of my ways and got busy replacing the lost value.

> **▼ TIP: Don't react emotionally to the events of Wall Street.**

Individual Plans

There are a number of ways you can set aside money for retirement that are independent of any company for which you work. These personal retirement vehicles allow you to make annual tax-deductible contributions. The accounts must meet IRS Code 408 requirements, but are created and funded at the discretion of the employee. They are not employer-sponsored plans, so it's up to you (using the guidance of your financial adviser) to find and fund the plan that will maximize your income in retirement.

An Individual Retirement Account (IRA) functions as a tax-deferred means of setting aside money for retirement. By federal law, you are able to contribute up to $2,000 annually and, depending on how much you earn and your marital status, the money you invest may or may not be tax-deductible. There are several types of IRAs: Traditional IRA, Roth IRA, Education IRA (EDIRA), SEP-IRA, SARSEP-IRA, and the SIMPLE IRA. Your professional broker will be happy to discuss each of these vehicles. Understand and consider these vehicles, especially if you are looking at self-employment as a means of walking away from the corporate grind. (If this is the case, you will likely need to find a new home for your retirement account(s) built up with your past employer.) Each of these IRAs offers a slightly different set of rules and terms, but the best part of all is your IRA grows tax-free just like your before-tax investments through your employer. Tax-free growth is a good thing; make sure you place this at the top of your investment strategy until you become eligible to withdraw funds or are forced to because you have reached age 70.

The following brief description explains each IRA and some basic differentiating characteristics.

■ The **Traditional IRA** is a tax-deferred personal retirement fund. You can contribute up to $2,000 a year before taxes, depending on marital status and income. Check with your tax professional for the rules. This vehicle is available to all working personnel and their spouses. This is the vehicle into which you might opt to roll over a retirement account like a 401(k) or 403(b) from a previous employer.

■ The **Roth IRA** is a tax-deferred retirement plan named for William Roth, longtime federal legislative friend to the saver. The Roth IRA is a tax-deferred retirement account that turns the traditional IRA formula in reverse: contributions are after-tax dollars, and withdrawals are completely tax free when you reach age 59 1/2, provided you have held the Roth IRA for five years. There are certain conversion provisions for turning your traditional IRA into a Roth IRA. While the Roth IRA sounds extremely attractive up front, make sure you understand all the rules and deal with a licensed investment adviser as well as consult your tax professional.

■ **EDITA or the Education IRA** lets you contribute up to $500 each year for anyone younger than 18. When the beneficiary withdraws the money to pay for qualified education expenses, the withdrawals generally are tax free.

■ The **SEP-IRA**, or Simplified Employee Pension IRA, is a tax-deferred retirement plan provided for sole proprietors or small businesses, most of which do not have other retirement vehicles. The difference in the SEP-IRA over a traditional IRA is the ability for the employer to contribute up to 15 percent of an employee's total compensation to a maximum of $25,500. Withstanding these higher contribution limits, the rules are generally the same as the traditional IRA. These funds grow tax-free until time of withdrawal, and then are taxed as ordinary income. Should an employee decide to leave a company offering a SARSEP-IRA and he is vested, this type of retirement plan can be rolled over into a traditional IRA.

■ **SARSEP-IRA,** or the Salary Reduction Simplified Employee Pension IRA, is a tax-deferred retirement plan provided by sole proprietors or small business with 25 or fewer employees. Both the employer and/or the employee make the SARSEP-IRA investment contribution to an employee's account. The investment grows tax-free until withdrawal, when it is treated as ordinary income (like any other IRA). Should an employee decide to leave a company offering a SARSEP-IRA and he is vested, this type of retirement plan can be rolled over into a traditional IRA.

■ **SIMPLE-IRA,** or the Savings Incentive Match Plan for Employees, actually replaced the SARSEP-IRA plan for those plans initiated after Jan. 1, 1997. The only real difference is the SIMPLE-IRA may now service an employer with up to 100 employees who do not maintain or contribute to any other plan; otherwise the rules are generally the same.

■ Finally, the **Keogh** plan is a tax-deferred retirement plan designed to help self-employed workers or individuals who earn self-employed income to establish a retirement savings plan. There are two basic types of plans: the profit-sharing plan and the money-purchase plan. Under Keogh regulations, the money-purchase contribution is mandatory. You must make the same percentage contribution each year whether you make a profit or not. The profit-sharing plan, on the other hand, allows for a change in percentage each year. Individuals may contribute to both types of plans in the same year. The most attractive feature to the Keogh plan is the high maximum contribution allowed. The contribution and the investment growth are tax-deferred until withdrawal; then the withdrawal is taxed as ordinary income.

As stated many times, the description of these plans is for informational purposes only. Make sure that your financial future is entrusted to a professional licensed investment adviser. While you fund these plans individually, you don't need to be making the decisions alone.

Employee-Sponsored Plans

A second set of retirement planning options, funded through a partnership between you and your employer, is available: the

Defined Benefit Plan and the Defined Contribution Plan. In the **Defined Benefit Plan**, an employer pays a set amount to participants each year based on a pre-determined formula, like length of service and the average income of the individual during the last five years. The Pension Benefit Guaranty Corporation (PBGC), a federal agency much like the Federal Deposit Insurance Corporation, which protects your savings in member banks, insures the defined benefit plan. The PBGC will guarantee your monthly pension up to $3,051.14, for a worker who retires at age 65. Should you retire before age 65, the amount will be less.

This type of defined benefit plan tends to reward the loyal employee, usually requiring some term of eligibility to be fully vested, possibly after five, seven, or ten years of uninterrupted employment. However, these pensions are non-transferable. Should you leave your job or be terminated, your pension benefit is forfeited. If you work in a particularly volatile industry known for upheavals and heavy feast-or-famine cycles, such as the technology industry, the pension or defined benefit plan would not be as attractive as a defined contribution plan.

The **Defined Contribution Plan**, such as a 401(k), is an employer-sponsored plan in which contributions are made to individual participant accounts, and the final benefit consists solely of assets (including investment returns) that have accumulated in these individual accounts. Depending on the type of defined contribution plan, contributions may be made either by the company, the participant, or both.

For most people, the 401(k) is the most attractive retirement plan because of its portability and tax-deferred status. The individual contributes pre-taxed dollars to his 401(k). If you are in a 28 percent tax bracket, you have saved an additional $28 for every $100 saved. A lot of workers fail to fully utilize this opportunity. It's like having an ice cream cone on a hot summer day and letting it melt in the sun. Not fully utilizing this retirement option through your company-sponsored plan is foolhardy, especially if you are caught up in excessive credit card debt and paying outrageous interest that could be going to your future.

Qualifying plans receive favorable tax treatment by meeting

the requirements of section 401(a) of the Internal Revenue Code and by following applicable regulations. Today, more than 40 million people in the United States have 401(k) plans for retirement. The average employee's plan is $50,000 and ranks as the number two investment vehicle outside his home.

The term 401(k) actually refers to a section of the tax code generated by the Employee Retirement Income Security Act of 1974 (ERISA). 401(k) type plans and IRAs came into existence by legislative action. They were introduced because of concerns about Social Security's ability to meet the needs of retired workers in the future. In the 1970s it became apparent that, because of zero population growth and an ever-increasing life expectancy, Social Security would be unable to fund the needs of a boomer population.

> ▼ **TIP: For most people, the 401(k) is the most attractive retirement plan.**

This forward thinking by our elected officials in Washington has had one of the most profound impacts on the American economy, even the world economy. The effects of defined contribution plans introduced in the 1970s are the primary reason for the significant economic growth experienced in the previous decade in the United States.

The 401(k) plan is for employees of for-profit entities. It is sponsored by the employer and usually administered by a large financial institution, known as a service provider—a company that provides any type of service to the plan, including managing assets, record keeping, providing plan education, and administering the plan. Service providers and plan sponsors are required by law to design and administer their plans in accordance with ERISA.

Among its statutes, ERISA calls for proper plan reporting and disclosure to participants. The individual plan must include an ERISA Rights Statement that explains the participant and beneficiary rights and must be included within a summary plan description (SPD).

Tax Sheltered Annuities (TSA), also known as a 403(b) plan, provide a tax shelter for 501(c)(3) tax-exempt employers (which include public schools). Employers qualifying for a TSA may defer taxes on contributions to certain annuity contracts or custodial accounts.

Employers often offer contributions to the defined contribution plan as a benefit, but there is a hitch. Sometimes, the vesting of these employer contributions is tied to the employee's time of service with the company. The structure for determining your right to company contributions that have accrued in your individual account in called the vesting schedule.

In a plan with immediate vesting, company contributions are fully vested as soon as they are deposited to a participant's account. Cliff vesting means company contributions will be fully vested only after a specific amount of time; employees who leave before this happens will not be entitled to any of the company contributions (with certain exceptions for retirees). In plans with graduated vesting, vesting occurs in specified increments.

Know the rules of your plan and make sure you understand what is yours when you leave. An employer contribution is a nice benefit, but should you be inclined to move from employer to employer, the contribution reduces the amount of tax-deferred dollars you could have saved independently. And you might not have experienced the maximum amount allowable because of an employer contribution you never stayed long enough to realize.

With all this consideration for the future, what happens when the future has snuck up on you? A participant might be allowed to withdraw his pension plan contributions in a defined contribution plan prior to retirement due to an explainable hardship or through the compliance of Form 72T. Hardship distributions are taxable as early withdrawals and are subject to a 10 percent penalty tax if the participant is less than age 59 1/2. The 72T classification can bypass the penalty portion of the withdrawal, but be advised, there are several hitches in the process, like staging your withdrawals over a specific period based on certain actuarial tables. Make sure you have discussed this move with your tax and financial professionals.

There are many examples of variations on these defined plans, such as an ESOP (employee stock ownership plan). The ESOP is a qualified defined contribution plan in which plan assets are invested primarily or exclusively in the securities of the sponsoring employer. In many instances these plans have paid handsomely, and in some instances individuals lost everything, including dollars they rolled over from previous employers. The ESOP plan has many merits, but be wary of having all your eggs in one basket.

> ▼ **TIP: Limit your exposure to your employer's stock.**

The best advice is to limit your exposure to your employer's stock. In the fall of 2000, Enron, the large Houston-based energy concern, was flying high; its stock was trading at more than $90 per share. It was the seventh-largest company on the Fortune 500.

Today, thanks in part to its financial missteps, Enron looks to be one of the biggest bankruptcy cases of all time. Enron employees have been devastated. Sixty percent of the firm's 401(k) was in Enron stock. To add insult to injury, Enron's plan was locked down at its collapse, so employees were not allowed to sell shares. The moral of the story is: Never keep more than 10 percent of your retirement plan in employer stock.

When looking at anyone's financial future, especially when a spouse is in the picture, understand the **Qualified Domestic Relations Order** (QDRO), in which a judgment, decree, or order creates or recognizes the right of an alternate payee (such as former spouse, child, etc.) to receive all or a portion of a participant's retirement plan benefits.

In the event of a divorce or domestic situation, the plan might have to be split between two or more individuals. The funds can be dispersed easily without tax or penalty, so long as funds are moved to a qualified plan. See your tax and investment professional for assistance.

Social Security

The idea of Social Security came into existence in a speech Franklin Delano Roosevelt made to Congress on July 8, 1934. America was attempting to pull out of the Great Depression; many workers had lost everything because of bank closures and failed businesses. Social Security was meant to offer workers some monetary retirement guarantee as well as protect widows and orphans of deceased workers.

▼ **TIP: Should you change jobs in any given year and your earning exceeds the maximum amount for Social Security for that given year, you might be eligible to a refund through your income tax filing.**

The Social Security Act of 1935 paid its first benefit to Ida Mae Fuller, a retired legal secretary in Vermont. That first check was for the sum of $22. According to Social Security Administration lore, Ms. Fuller would go on to receive more than $22,000 in benefits until her death in 1975.

Today, Social Security protects retirement for 150 million workers while paying benefits to 45 million retirees. The current Social Security plan calls for workers to contribute 7.45 percent of their wages up to $80,400, while employers match that amount.

You are probably wondering whether you will ever see anything from Social Security, especially considering what you have contributed over your career and what the media have stirred up in your mind. The answer to what we will actually receive is far more complicated than we might expect. Until the 1980s, a person was eligible to take early retirement with reduced benefits at age 62, and 65 was considered the age for retirement at which full benefits were available. However, advances in health care have extended the lives of workers, directly affecting Social Security. Today the Social Security Administration uses a sliding scale for extending the age at which a worker is eligible for full retirement benefits. For instance, I must wait to retire until age 67. You may visit the Social Security website, www.ssa.gov for help in determining your eligibility date so you can plan accordingly for your retirement. Be prepared to contact SSA at least three months before retirement for timely benefit payments. The phone number is (800) 772-1213. Social Security's retirement benefits are paid not only to workers but also to their spouses (including divorced spouses) and their dependents at a defined time.

> ▼ **TIP: When planning your retirement package, make sure you have balanced it with individual and employer-sponsored plans to supplement the Social Security earnings you will receive. The right mix of options is vital to having a secure retirement.**

In addition to Social Security, your family will be eligible for Supplemental Security Income (SSI) if you are injured or die. SSI is an insurance plan designed to offer income protection in the event that a worker becomes injured leading to disability and is available until age 65. The level of earnings the worker was making determines the benefit. Today, SSI protects 5 million disabled workers and 1.6 million dependents.

Cashing Out

When it's time to move on, whether it's an involuntary reduction or you choose to leave your employer, you need to consider your options for whether to cash out your retirement plan. If the plan is a defined benefit plan (pension plan), your options are limited; usually you leave that type of plan behind. If the plan is a defined contribution plan, then you may choose to roll a qualified plan over into another plan or you may cash out the plan.

These cash-outs are subject to federal withholding tax, and are subject to the 10 percent early withdrawal penalty if not rolled over into a qualified plan within 60 days. Make sure you discuss this with your human resources personnel before you leave. One simple rollover solution is to open an IRA, either online or by visiting a financial service center for a large brokerage firm such as Fidelity, Schwab, or even your insurance agent's office.

The frequency with which younger workers are cashing out of 401(k) plans when they leave a job is disturbing. A Hewitt study found that 68 percent took a cash-out when changing jobs, while 26 percent chose to roll over the balance into a qualified plan, and only 6 percent transferred the balance to a new employer.

It is estimated that younger workers will change jobs nine times over their careers. If a worker opts to "cash out" of his 401(k) plan each time, he will be paying excessive taxes and penalties over his lifetime. We make the following scenario for not cashing out: a 32-year-old planning to cash out a $10,000 401(k) would actually receive only $5,500 after taxes and penalties. That same $10,000, growing tax-free at 12 percent (the historical rate of return of the S&P) without another contribution, would yield $300,000 at age 62. Consider the long-term consequences to your retirement before you seek the short-term gain.

Life and Disability Insurance

Now that you've prepared for your retirement, it's time to consider planning for your family should something happen to you. One of the biggest concerns facing workers with families and dependents is what happens in the worker's absence.

If you are employed, you may well have access to disability and accidental death insurance through your employer. Life insurance often is included in any benefits packages offered by most employers. Policies tend to vary from a basic $10,000 group term policy to as much as 2.5 times your annual compensation. But should you become disabled, you are likely to lose your employer's life insurance and accidental death benefit.

How much life insurance is enough? Make sure you have three to five times your last five years' average annual wage in independent insurance coverage, meaning, not company sponsored. Many corporations today will offer one to two times your salary as a benefit at a phenomenally discounted rate. If you have the option to add additional coverage, do it. It's inexpensive compared with insurance on the open market. Also make sure you have a policy or two on the side, just in case you lose your job. I recommend getting additional coverage in at least two separate policies. As your net worth and financial portfolio grow, your need to have replacement income declines. The two-policy concept then allows you to drop a policy as needed or when it gets too costly, especially in the case of term insurance. Spend time now with a professional insurance representative planning for your future. As we age,

> ▼ **TIP: The longer you wait to acquire additional insurance, the more it will cost, including not being able to qualify for adequately priced coverage.**

it is important to understand those benefits and arrange for any additional coverage. The longer you wait to acquire additional insurance, the more it will cost.

SSI is not the only disability insurance available. Your employer often offers short-term disability coverage as well as long-term disability coverage. Short-term coverage is available after an employee misses work because of illness for five to ten business days. Many larger corporations tend to self-insure this benefit; they pay all claims by employees in regular payroll and at the end of some time period, they might have an agreement or policy with a re-insurer or underwriter who will reimburse the company over a certain amount paid in short-term benefits. Short-term benefits typically run 90 days but might vary based on state or local statutes. The actual benefit paid might be anywhere from 40 percent to 100 percent of salary and benefits during this period likely will require some sort of documentation from a licensed healthcare provider.

Long-term disability insurance through your employer typically goes into effect where short-term leaves off and is usually available only to personnel working full time. The benefit for this type of insurance usually complements any SSI benefits. Let's say you earn $8,000 a month. Your benefit package states you are eligible for 66 percent of your usual and customary or monthly earnings, or $5,280 per month, until you recover, the term of the benefit expires, you reach a stated cap in the benefit policy, or you reach retirement age. Let's say you also are eligible for $1,360 per month SSI (Social Security Insurance) benefit. Your eligible benefit will be reduced by that SSI amount; the long-term disability benefits payable through your employer's benefit is $3,920.

Benefits in Transition

The only thing that's certain in the Networked Economy is rapid change. Statistics show that today's workers will change jobs up to eight times and careers one to two times before they retire. The time to prepare for the transition is now—before it happens. In the midst of an impending job terminations, it is important to have a cash reserve to fall back on. Present-day diviners are saying six to nine months of reserves should be adequate, which might seem steep but is necessary. Most employees, when surveyed about their knowledge of benefits in a layoff, believed that severance pay was mandatory. It is not. Companies are not required to offer severance pay. Consider anything you might get as goodness.

Considering the extreme economic conditions when this book was written, the rule of thumb for judging the time to gain re-employment is up to one year for every $100,000 in income, so if you make $80,000 a year, nine months is pretty near what you will need. Should you find yourself caught up in excessive credit card debt, take heed. There is light at the end of the tunnel. Current calculations estimate that the $1,000 outstanding balance you maintain will only take thirty-some-odd years to pay off using the minimum payment method. If this is the case and you and your spouse are buried in high interest debt, you are facing the number one reason most marriages fail. Get it under control, see a credit counselor, toss those credit cards away, and drop the impulsive spending habits. Credit counselors are often available at no charge to you; they are sometimes compensated by the creditor involved for putting you on track and lowering their risk of your debt. Get help; don't let this take you down the drain. If you are laid off, this debt gnaws on your every nerve.

> ▼ **TIP: The rule of thumb for judging the time to gain re-employment is up to one year for every $100,000 in income.**

It is important to know which retirement and insurance benefits go with you and which benefits you lose. There are laws that protect you in the event of a job loss, divorce, or loss of sufficient hours of weekly or monthly employment to remain eligible for coverage. Your health insurance coverage—including mental health, vision, and dental—is available for up to 18 months at the same cost your employer was getting the coverage for. The means by which this coverage is available is the Consolidated Omnibus Budget Reconciliation Act of 1985 or COBRA.

COBRA includes a continuation of health coverage under certain qualifying events when your coverage through a company-sponsored plan ends. Qualified beneficiaries include employees who were previously covered by their company and dependent spouses and children of a covered employee.

A qualifying event is any of the following:

■ Voluntary or involuntary termination of employee's employment.

■ Reduction in the hours of employment to non-eligible status.

■ An employee, spouse, or dependent becomes eligible for Medicare.

■ Divorce or legal separation.

■ Death of an employee or spouse and the loss of dependent status by a child.

The coverage sponsor, in conjunction with the employer, is required to notify the qualified individual of his eligibility within 14 days of a qualifying event. COBRA continuation coverage may be elected up to 60 days after:

■ Coverage ends due to a qualifying event.

■ Notice of COBRA continuation coverage is provided to the qualified beneficiary.

Premiums cannot exceed 102 percent of the plan's full cost of coverage for other beneficiaries not covered by COBRA. The initial premium (cost of coverage) is due 45 days after the date of the COBRA election, and monthly payments are generally due on or about the same day of each month. Prices generally remain fixed for the length of eligibility as long as the previous cost was lower than permitted by law at the time that a disability extension is engaged (see plan), or the beneficiary opts to change coverage options.

> ▼ **TIP: In the event of a job loss, expect your COBRA benefits to be quite expensive. You might want to investigate a personal policy on your own.**

Length of coverage depends on the type of qualifying event and the status of the beneficiary. For termination of employment or the reduction of hours of employment, coverage usually lasts 18 months. When a dependent of a qualified employee reaches age of qualification for Medicare before the employee does, the maximum length of coverage is 36 months.

Your COBRA will likely offer you some conversion option for life insurance; you can exchange this benefit for an individual insurance policy. Make sure you do your homework; this might be a good time to shop for life insurance. This conversion effort generally falls outside the typical interpretation of COBRA guidelines; so these conversion-type policies often include a lengthy medical questionnaire, review of medical history, or an actual medical examination at the expense of the issuing company.

If, according to Title II or XVI of the Social Security Act, you are disabled at the time of the qualifying event that starts COBRA coverage, you are eligible for an 11-month disability extension to the usual 18-month eligibility. Otherwise disability insurance will usually cease when you are no longer employed. When dealing with qualification of Social Security disability, confer with your physician and seek adequate legal counsel specializing in disability determination; it can save you a lot of headaches and heartaches.

Family and Medical Leave Act

Events can, and do, occur that require you to temporarily suspend active employment. You may have to care for a child who has become ill, an aged parent, spouse, significant other, or life partner who is in need of temporary, continuous supervision or care. You are eligible for insurance coverage as well as time to tend these loved ones. The Family and Medical Leave Act makes some provisions for insurance coverage.

Consider your legal rights surrounding the Family and Medical Leave Act (FMLA Public Law 103-3 or any local, state, or governing law) and understand your insurance coverage and/or the continuation of coverage throughout the period of the leave. Most company human resources manuals and human resources staff personnel or employer-sponsored benefits website spell out your rights to coverage. It also might be worthwhile to investigate the tax-free spending account provision portion of your overall compensation.

Contact any equivalent local government agency or your

state's Department of Labor for copies of laws ruling FMLA. Make sure that your specific situation is covered, especially where parents, stepchildren, significant others, and life partners are concerned. Know your rights and be prepared.

Conclusion

Managing finances and benefits in today's complex world requires knowledge and time. As you focus on creating value in the Networked Economy, you need the help of a team that is focused on your financial goals and well-being. Make sure you select your team members carefully and routinely meet with them to discuss the things that have changed in your personal situation.

Survival Tips

■ Keep a reserve of cash—six to nine months' salary is a good starting point.

■ If you don't have one, get an investment adviser.

■ Leverage your investment adviser to stay educated on financial options.

■ Keep abreast of your employer-sponsored benefits.

Questions for Consideration

■ Do you have a financial planner and have you recently evaluated your retirement plan?

■ How much do you have in cash reserves?

■ Are you contributing the maximum in your 401(k) account?

■ Do you contribute to IRA accounts?

■ How much combined life insurance do you have (employer-sponsored and individual)?

■ Do you understand COBRA?

■ Do you understand your company's usual policy on severance?

■ Do you have a will or trust?

■ Have you considered organ donation? (Optional)

■ Do you understand the benefits of tax-deferred spending accounts?

▼

Planning Your Next Job

Until the late '80s and early '90s, industrial America as well as other industrialized nations looked at the worker as the basic component of commerce. If trained in a task-oriented fashion, little was left to error and the sum of the parts meant a more valuable whole. A very simple but effective system considering the times. But this also left the workers of the day not comprehending the near-term goals of the corporation and how the components actually came together for the benefit of an over-arching goal of the employer.

Today, it's more important than ever that you, the corporate citizen, completely understand your employer's long-term and short-term goals, market strategy, and overall value proposition. It is important to have passion about what you're doing, to take pride in the fact you are doing a job, and to fully understand why your job is critical to the overall well-being of your company. On the other hand, should you lack that passion, or not have that sense of accomplishment, it might be time to change jobs. You are in complete control of this scenario.

Then there is the unfortunate circumstance that your services might no longer be needed. Your employer has decided to sever its relationship with you. It possibly had nothing to do with you. You need to be ready for either instance.

No matter the circumstance, you need to be prepared to make this move. If you are caught off guard, you might not be as ready to make a jump as if you planned to change jobs. But being ready has many facets you must consider. Up to this point, we have addressed things like skills assessment with your current employer, understanding your true value to your employer, your personality, educational level, and some circumstances to expect in the future. These are all important aspects of being successful, but they also are critical for being prepared for a change. It is important that you continually stay on top of these issues as well as the remaining factors covered in this section.

Networking

The help of other people can be the single largest contributor to your productivity, whether on the job or in the process of finding suitable employment. The phrase "no man is an island" comes to mind when we think about the aspects of networking. Maintaining that close-knit network of friends, mentors, and co-workers is necessary to understand your value in this economy. Without the help and support of other people we will never know what we have not received from our jobs or what we can achieve over the life of our career.

Current findings indicate that about half of the typical person's ability to get things done in life is through relationships with other people. If we don't have that assistance, it doesn't mean we're not productive. It means we're not as productive as we could have been.

Networking is ageless. Since the caveman's time, we have been networking to accomplish tasks. (Have you ever made the comment about not re-inventing the wheel when taking on a task?) Isn't it easier to look for the efforts of another person to jumpstart your efforts to complete a task? Why go to the trouble of repeating someone else's mistakes?

Are you the type of individual who will sit down and start a project without a plan? I remember getting a new gas grill for Father's Day. It came unassembled and I immediately took to the daunting task to getting it over with. This truly looked easy, but that ended up being the wrong attitude. Had I taken the time to review the instructions, I might have saved an hour or two.

We can all benefit from the association with others. Human beings are always networking. To effectively enhance your productivity, you should take advantage of networking.

The concept of "Six Degrees of Separation" speaks well with how we interact with others. People interact with only six levels of separation at a maximum—think in terms of a friend of a friend of a friend, and so on.

When I was in elementary school, my father caught me shunning a student in a younger grade. He told me that, as I grew up, I would understand the importance of making friends my own age as well as friends who are older and younger. I understood the "older" part with mentors and all that stuff. The same age part was easy to understand, but I was stymied about making friends with people younger than I was.

> ▼ **TIP: To effectively enhance your productivity, take advantage of networking.**

I really began to understand this when my father passed away after a long illness. Most of his older friends had either passed away before him or were in ill health as well. However, a friend who was younger than my dad was very valuable in looking in on my mother. I'm sure this younger man did this out of respect for my dad as well as being one of those truly genuine and sincere people who inhabit this earth.

Networking has proven to be a valuable resource, even to the extent that organizations have sprung up far and wide with the honest intent of getting people together, whether they are entrepreneurs looking to meet others for the purpose of self-promotion, similarly linked corporate employees gathering within trade associations and professional groups, or, as of late, groups of unemployed people staying active while looking for jobs.

These are great opportunities for like-minded people to get together to trade, barter, discuss, and help one another. Take advantage of these organizations and events, join in, make contacts, and stay in touch with those you meet. It is what you make of these opportunities that counts.

Networking Etiquette

Manners are one of those things that often get overlooked when opportunity knocks; after all, business is business. The opportunities to network, schmooze, cavort, or rub elbows with opportunity exist every day.

Being active in these organizations, attending professional groups, joining local service organizations, and volunteering to hold office or lead trade associations is important to your future. However getting involved in these groups does not give you license to extend the effects of the group beyond their boundaries. Having belonged to the same church for more than a decade, I have seen far too many times when individuals overstepped the bounds of etiquette, thinking that membership granted them license to pillage other members for personal gain. I do not care to count the offers to review my life insurance needs, to join service organizations bent on saving the world, or help me understand the complexities of my financial morass.

There are manners to be deployed in networking; for example, passing out business cards at a wake is not appropriate. Here are some guidelines from several networking organizations:

■ At company or industry events, do not stand in the corner—mingle, reach out to strangers, be helpful, and *smile*.

■ Do not use voicemail messages for networking if you can help it. Attempt to have a live conversation, but keep it short.

■ Learn to ask open-ended questions, not ones that result in "yes" or "no" answers.

■ Be sure to express your thanks for the opportunity to meet someone. Send a note or e-mail.

■ If you commit to something, follow through. There is nothing worse than someone telling you he was going to do something and not do it.

These guidelines are important, especially if you are looking for a job. First impressions are everything. If you follow the rules of simple etiquette, you will not disappoint anyone in the process: a valuable contact, a prospective employer, or yourself.

When attending networking events, especially ones that are

for the specific purpose of finding a job, be prepared. Have your best foot forward. Do not underdress or overdress. If your particular position traditionally calls for a suit and tie, then wear one, no matter what the usual and customary event calls for. Make sure that fragrances and jewelry are muted, and men, shine your shoes.

It will be important to have that résumé handy. Don't work the room passing out your pedigree as though it were a flier at a sporting event, but be prepared. Have résumés in a portfolio along with several writing instruments and paper for notes. Your portfolio should be conservative without any company logos. There are numerous varieties available, including inexpensive vinyl "pleather" coated. The multiple writing instruments are important. I have been without a pen many times when I needed it most. If you have a nice pen, keep it in your pocket.

> ▼ **TIP: When attending networking events, be prepared.**

Have some generic ballpoint pens available to give a prospective employer or valuable contact to draw a map, make a note, or jot down a phone number.

Your manners are a direct reflection of the level of quality with which you will pursue a job. Being overly aggressive can be a detriment. I have seen individuals seem overly desperate, even to the point that I could almost smell their eagerness on their breath. Being aggressive is not a bad thing, but be sure to do it in a quality manner. Take the time to assess your audience at a networking type meeting. Try to understand who is attending a networking event. Understand who your competition is and how you might differentiate yourself from them. Be ready to discuss your background, experience, references, and salary requirements. Be careful to not be guilty of boasting, name-dropping, being overbearing or loud and imposing. This is the time you want to be thought of as the person a contact might want to take home to meet the family. Watch your manners.

Beyond networking and being prepared, I will refrain from the usual and customary skills for interviewing and résumé writing. If you find yourself needing some tips on interviewing, get with a friend or colleague, buy a good book or search the Internet. Résumé writing is a skill that every corporate citizen should be proficient at. It is your opportunity to sell yourself. If you are waiting until you are out of work to bring a résumé together, you have cheated yourself. Your résumé should be like your passport, always up to date and ready to go. With computers as accessible as they are today, there is no excuse for not having a fairly current résumé on hand. If you have a computer entrusted to you at work, have a copy there, provided it is not in violation of company policy. Be ready to promote yourself at the drop of a hat; make people remember you.

> **▼ TIP: Your résumé should be like your passport, always up to date and ready to go.**

Becoming a Free Agent

There was a time when I thought I might have grown old at a certain employer. I had grown quite accustomed to the way things were. After all, I had personally been responsible for the annualized growth of the company (or so I believed). Suddenly, the management team I had grown so accustomed to for seven years was gone. I immediately butted heads with the new manager—I had lost my power base. The problem was mine, not his, but I made my decisions based on my ego rather than common sense.

This was the beginning of a lesson that took several years to learn. In hindsight, I realize that I had probably stayed too long, but that's water over the dam. It was getting tougher to compete in the part of the industry I had grown up in—margins were getting squeezed and the grass was looking greener elsewhere. I chose to jump ship and join the number two vendor in a given industry segment. I thought it would be easy: These guys were hot and they had recently made a significant acquisition. Little did I know that the guy I replaced had apparently set fire to every bridge he had crossed in my new assignment. At the same time, the industry was polarizing between factions beyond my control. The wheels where falling off. I saw the handwriting on the wall, but I hung in there. Before I knew it, I was running down leads and closing business left on the table by my predecessors. This proved to be very rewarding finan-cially, so I made it work while I continued to look for a new oppor-tunity. I was able to continue with this group for a year or so until the poor financial performance of the company became unbearable and a new suitor appeared. I was quick to jump to the leading company in the sector. Little did I know, I had just joined the ranks of free agency. I was hired to do a job, I did it, and there was no reason to stay after the work was done.

> ▼ **TIP:**
> **Working as an independent contractor is a good way to leverage your skills in the networked economy.**

Professional sports players fig-ured this out long ago. While they are at the top of their game, they have the ability to jump from team to team. These athletes are engaged heavily in career planning. They are playing for bigger stakes than the typical corporate citizen, but they also have a much shorter career life expectancy.

Are you beginning to think like a free agent? Do you have any restrictions holding you back? Mid-life corporate citizens have this serious entrepreneurial spirit that rears its ugly head fre-quently. Proceed cautiously in making this type of move, but the current economy is primed for independence. There is a lot of work to be done, and jobs will be plentiful, just not necessarily on a permanent full-time basis. Blue-collar trades people associated with construction have been doing business this way for years. Working as an independent contractor is a good way to leverage your skills in the Networked Economy.

Explore your value in this economy and assess whom you

might be able to engage as customers. You might be able to continue doing your present job for your present employer as a contractor. This is a serious consideration to make because many things change when you decide to depart the security of the mother ship. Weigh the costs and the benefits carefully.

Corporations in the 21st century will be more virtual than ever before; one day you are a user, next you are a customer, then possibly a contributing consultant. It is important that you understand where you fit in this new way of doing business. Your ability to play a virtual role is key; it is up to you, however, to decide whether you are permanent or part time.

If you go out on your own, you need to expect some stagnancy. Business might be slow to catch on but watch—it will zoom. Being in the right time at the right place is not all that is needed here; you need the right components for growth. And you need to consider how you can juggle several companies' needs if you are able to attract additional business. It will take considerable effort to keep these components pointed in the right direction.

Make Sure You Get It In Writing

I'm reminded about an opportunity my older brother had when he joined an Australian recycled paper manufacturer as its head of sales. He was smart enough to have a lawyer draft an employment agreement. This paper recycler was in the middle of the timber belt, attempting to compete with an inexpensive, newly manufactured, better quality product. When the holding company opted to change the business model (better described as cutting its losses), my brother's position was eliminated. Forty-eight hours after signing his termination paperwork, he had one year's total compensation in hand, delivered by courier. Good for him, a job well done.

Employment agreements are always good ideas, yet most employers do not offer them. If you can get your employer to offer one, more power to you. Employment agreements are useful but generally contain enough situational clauses that an employer might not have a problem wiggling out if it so chooses. You will often encounter the term "at will" employment. A stipulation found in many employment agreements, referenced in employee manuals, and contained in letters of offer is "at will." "At will" employment insinuates that an employee works at the will of the employer.

Employers tend to use this provision to avoid claims of unlawful termination by employees. Use of the "at will" phrase puts the responsibility on the terminated employee to prove that he or she had reasons to believe the employment was considered permanent. Employers will use the "at will" phrase to claim they can terminate any employee at any time, without reason. There is generally little that can be done in the event that you have signed a document acknowledging that you have been told your employer is an "at will" employer. This is generally contained in the statement preceding the signature blank on an employment application. Most employers will not even speak with a prospective employee without having a signed application. Make sure you are aware of what you are signing and if there is anything you question, line through it, initial it, and proceed.

The employment agreement is a written document between an employer and employee that establishes terms of employment. The employment agreement is designed to protect both parties. The promises contained in the agreement should contain all promises made prior to employment. Use of this instrument prevents any alleged claims of verbal promises, so make sure that anything you discussed prior to employment is contained in the document. The typical corporate employment agreement might include the following provisions:

- Job description, including duties and responsibilities for the employee
- Job performance expectations and description of evaluation criteria
- Length of time or completion of milestone in which agreement will be in force
- Compensation, including fixed, incentive, optional, deferred, equity, and ownership
- Expenses and out-of-pocket costs that are eligible for reimbursement

■ Implications regarding the change in health of the employee

■ Implications in change of ownership of the employer

■ Secrecy statements and expectations of remedy for violation

■ Loyalty statement and expectations of the employer

■ Anti-competition provisions, including the names of those companies deemed to be competitors

■ Company property use and its demise upon termination or separation

■ Termination provisions, severance, benefits, accrued holiday pay, expense reimbursements, and references for eligibility for future employment

Oral or Implied Contracts

Implied contracts happen in many ways and are far more common than written contracts in employment matters. Implied or oral contracts can be created in two ways: by oral statements and by implication, meaning the evidence of a contract was implied. Implied contracts evolve in several ways. They are justified through any and all of the following: length of service, disciplinary policy, and benefit offerings. The employee who has served an employer for a number of years, who has had no real disciplinary action brought against him or documented action that was labeled disciplinary combined with the continued offer of benefits can often be construed as an implied employment contract. But do not trust that this implied arrangement will get you anywhere in the event of a planned termination.

Trade Secrets

Employers are demanding more than ever that employees agree with specific trade secret requirements as terms of employment. In most states, a trade secret is where the owner of the trade secret maintains a competitive advantage over other companies by virtue of the item in question.

The trade secret is generally kept protected from:

■ Public disclosure

■ Companies doing business in the same general area of interest

■ Competitive marketplace of the trade secret owner

Some illustrations of trade secrets include a formula or concoction, a method of gathering information or data, a new product prior to filing for a patent, methods for market penetration strategies, specific recipes or compilation of ingredients, specialized manufacturing processes, and software source code.

> ▼ **TIP: Several states have also enacted laws making trade secret infringement a crime.**

Trade secrets are a self-policing form of protection. Trade secrets are not registered with any governmental agency; it's the employer's responsibility to keep the information private, including marking those items as such.

Trade secret protection generally is expected to last for as long as the secret is kept private. However, many employers ask that these secrets be protected for up to five years after an employee leaves a company or the secret is made available to the public. From this point, the employer generally protects its interest with patents, trademarks, and copyrights.

In the late '70s and early '80s, a great deal of Apple computer's technology was actually devised and created at Xerox Palo Alto Research Center in California. Many former employees of Xerox PARC made their way to Apple, down the street in Cupertino, Calif. But Xerox owned the burden of proof about any trade secret violations.

So let's say you have, in fact, pirated a trade secret from an employer. You can expect an immediate injunction from a ruling court to appear immediately. From there, you can expect a good deal of questioning. The deliberate theft of your employer's trade secrets can constitute federal and state crimes.

The most significant federal law dealing with trade secret

theft is the Economic Espionage Act of 1996. The EEA punishes intentional stealing, copying, or receiving of trade secrets "related to or included in a product that is produced for or placed in interstate commerce."

Several states have also enacted laws making trade secret infringement a crime. For example, in California it is a crime to acquire, disclose, or use trade secrets without authorization. Violators may be fined up to $5,000, sentenced to up to one year in jail, or both.

Valued Assets

Your company's two most valuable assets are its trade secrets and employees. Many employers are intent on protecting these assets from the following:

- An employee starting a competing business
- An employee going to work for a competitor
- An ex-employee soliciting your customers
- An ex-employee recruiting your current employees
- An ex-employee divulging your trade secrets, processes, customer lists or ideas to a competitor

No-compete agreements may not be enforceable in some states (for instance, California) or have special rules (such as Florida, Texas, and Louisiana). When departing a company for a new, similar employer, check with legal counsel and let your future employer know about any agreements you have signed regarding competitive practices.

Most prospective employers do not want you to bring any trade secrets or intellectual property with you for fear of a lawsuit. Generally, they will inquire when you start work about property both physical and intellectual that might be considered secret by your previous employer. They will ask you to return it, subject to termination in the event that their wishes have not been complied with.

Take heed; what you believe is idiotic can be the basis for a lengthy legal battle that a former employer will take quite seriously.

Background Checks

Depending on the information a prospective or existing employer plans to collect, it may conduct a background check. Generally, as long as the records checked are relevant to the job for which the employer is considering hiring a worker, the employer is on safe ground. However, state and federal laws restrict or prohibit employers from gathering or using certain types of records. Most employers considering running a background check will ask applicants and employees for consent to the check in advance, in writing. Many companies require you fill out an application for employment prior to meeting with anyone to discuss opportunities. These employment applications generally require a signature with a considerable amount of small print adjacent to it. This signature generally proves acceptance by the prospective employee to the terms of the company in the interview process. This usually includes a background check prior to making a job offer.

▼ **TIP: Most employers considering running a background check will ask applicants and employees for consent to the check in advance, in writing.**

I know of a situation in which a prospective employee at a large international company misrepresented the truth on his job application about degrees conferred. It seems that he was a few credits shy of actually receiving the degree he claimed to have. This could have been grounds for rescinding a verbal employment offer to him. Many larger employers have actually built this in to their process for screening future personnel.

Now let's look at a situation in which a company decides to do background checks on its existing employees. Possibly you have been in the employ of this company for a number of years and never had your background checked. Since Sept. 11, 2001, many companies have chosen to screen existing employees. Your academic credentials are one of the items they look for, and if those statements are false, it may be grounds for immediate termination. If you have a stellar record and reputation and are considered to be a contributor to the company, you are likely to survive, possibly receiving a reprimand or reduction in job classification. If the company is in the process of streamlining, then the odds are not good that you will keep your job.

Credential inflation was rampant in the last two decades. Employees jumped jobs, especially in such industries as technology, sales, and health care, as a means of getting that much deserved raise in pay or better yet, a signing bonus. Padding one's résumé was commonplace. As a hiring manager I saw plenty of evidence of people stretching the truth to get my attention. This is dangerous ground. Honesty is the best policy.

Your Financial History

An employer must get an employee's written consent before seeking your credit report—many employers include a request for such consent in their employment applications. Once they get the report, they can consider it in deciding whether to hire you. However, if you have not been hired based on information in the report, the prospective employer should give you a copy of the report or tell you where it can be obtained. The credit-reporting source usually has information readily available on how to challenge the report if need be.

Drug Testing

An employer can require drug testing if he has a reasonable suspicion that a particular employee is using drugs (if the employee has glassy or red eyes, concentration problems, or otherwise appears to be impaired at work, for example). The employer can also test for a drug if the company is filling a position that carries a high risk of injury or requires an employee to carry a weapon. Drug testing is for real; often, companies employed in contracts with governmental agencies are required to drug test. This is not something to take lightly. If you are currently taking prescription drugs that could be confused as an offending drug, say so. However, you might find that your assignment could be changed based on the degree of risk involved.

Collection Agencies

One of the nastiest groups of individuals in the world is collection agency personnel. They are some of the most irreverent human beings on the planet. These people are relentless, calling your place of employment, sometimes asking for the personnel department to start garnishment proceedings against your paycheck. Some tactics deployed by these collection agents often skirt the Fair Debt Collection Practices Act of 1996. The Federal Trade Commission oversees the policing of this act and can be engaged if you believe you have been abused or your rights have been violated.

A collection agency cannot contact you before 8 a.m. or after 9 p.m. Its personnel may not use profane language and they cannot make false claims or accusations. You may dispute the claim of collection and this actually stops the collection process for 30 days.

If the collection agency contacts you at work, you can simply tell them that company policy forbids personal phone calls and they are no longer able to call you there. Threats to garnish wages cannot be made without first having a court order and lastly, you can write the collection agency and enact the "shut up" privilege, in which the collection agency has one last opportunity to contact you stating its intentions. Check the Federal Trade Commission's website for more details on your rights, www.ftc.gov.

Debt rises dramatically when the economy sours. During the crash of the dot.coms, many employees were hounded by collection agencies due to unsecured debt incurred for business purposes. This debt was most likely incurred when a person might have unknowingly signed for an item or charged travel or other expenses on a company-issued credit card and the company was unable to reimburse the individual. You may very well owe the money, even if the company failed to reimburse you.

Psychological Tests

Although this is an unsettled area of law, it might depend on the test. Many widely used psychological tests ask questions that invade a test-taker's privacy. The jury is still out as to whether these tests have any ability to predict whether a particular employee will lie, steal, manage poorly, or cause other workplace problems. Because these tests are an imprecise measure at best, and because they are likely to be intrusive, employers would do well to avoid these tests in most circumstances. Should you believe that you have been discriminated against because of some poor result on a psychological test, seek the advice of an employment attorney, and then weigh the outcome of raising questions about decisions made through analysis of findings.

Personal Beliefs

An employer may not fire a worker because of his religious or political beliefs. Federal and state laws (and the First Amendment of the U.S. Constitution) protect workers from this type of discrimination. However, if a worker brings his beliefs into the workplace by, for example, attempting to convert other workers to his religion or publicizing his political beliefs during work time, the employer may put a stop to this.

Working for the Competition

The laws of many states prohibit marital status discrimination—discrimination against someone because she is married, single, or divorced. However, employers are not required to hire or promote a worker who, because of her spouse's job, might have a conflict of interest.

Invasion of Privacy

E-mail may be read, depending on the policies of the employer. If the company has a policy of e-mail privacy (if you have been told that your e-mail will be confidential or will not be read by the company, for example), then the company must abide by that policy. Also, if the company allows employees to designate certain messages as confidential or private, it shouldn't read those messages. Otherwise, the company has the right to monitor employee e-mail, as long as it has a legitimate business purpose for doing so.

Specific caution should be taken here; abide by the rules. If the company frowns on personal e-mail, *do not do it!* The company will use the e-mail if necessary in a litigation battle.

Your telephone calls can be listened to as well, with a few limitations. The employer is legally allowed to monitor employee conversations with customers for quality control. Federal law allows them to do so without warning or announcement, although some states require you to inform the parties to the call in some way that you might be listening. However, the employer may not monitor personal calls. Once an employer realizes that a call might be personal, he must stop monitoring.

> **▼ TIP: Understand the rules. Your employer most likely has the ability to monitor you. Be careful where you go on the Internet, who you e-mail with company property, and what you take to and from your place of employment.**

Searching employees when leaving the premises is usually a bad idea. Generally, employers can perform a workplace search in order to serve important, work-related interests—as long as they don't unduly intrude on the worker's privacy rights. Random searches are less likely to pass legal limits than a search of an employee suspected of theft. Should an employer have reasonable cause, he cannot conduct an invasive search: an employee's bag might be reasonable under some circumstances, but bodily contact searches of an employee are grounds for excessive force.

Camera for purposes of surveillance is appropriate depending on where the cameras are placed and why. The employer must have a reasonable basis for monitoring in this manner (to discourage theft from a cash register and enhance the security of customers, for example) and inform the employees of the cameras. Certain areas of the workplace (bathroom or changing areas) are generally off-limits to this type of monitoring.

Overtime

Federal law dictates that non-farm hour wage earning employees are entitled to at least one and one half times their hourly rate after either 40 hours in a given week or eight hours in a given day. There are instances where employees at Tyson Food, Wal-Mart, and Enterprise Rent-a-Car have taken their employers to task when expected to work off the clock or not be compensated for the time necessary to don proper attire for completion of their job. To compensate an employee for overtime with compensatory time off is not a good substitute. Federal law requires pay for overtime. In very limited situations, employers can give employees compensatory time off (commonly referred to as "comp time"). However, they must give this time off in the same pay period in which the overtime was worked, and you must give one and a half hours of comp time for every hour of overtime worked.

Management employees generally are not required to be paid overtime. Under federal law, executive, professional, and administrative employees are not entitled to overtime pay. An executive employee is one who routinely supervises two or more employees, has the right to hire, fire or promote workers, and routinely exercises discretion. An employee must spend at least 80 percent of the day engaged in these activities to qualify as an executive. So, if your managers supervise a department or group of employees and spend most of their days engaged in executive-level decision-making and activities, they are not entitled to overtime. But if you have simply tacked a glorified title onto an otherwise low-level job, you are required to pay overtime.

Certain commissioned sales people are eligible for overtime, but it really depends on what the employee makes. Retail and service establishments are not required to pay their commissioned employees overtime if the employee's regular rate of pay is more than one and a half times the minimum wage and if more than half the employee's pay comes from commissions. If your employees do not meet these requirements, you must pay them overtime.

In the event of an unexpected termination, when you are an hourly employee and you have routinely worked beyond the federal guidelines for regular time, you are entitled to compensation. Have some documented evidence of the time. Evidence can be as simple as a personal log, parking receipts, etc.

Vacation and Sick Leave

Many employees are surprised to learn that employers are not legally required to give their employees paid time off. Despite this legal flexibility, most employers do offer some variety of paid leave. Employers usually offer generous vacation and leave policies to attract high-quality employees and improve office productivity and morale.

If an employer decides to adopt a policy that gives employees paid vacation or sick time, the company must be sure to apply the policy consistently to all employees. Instances in which some employees might receive a more lucrative package than others might be grounds for a discrimination claim.

Getting Fired

Let's face it, a corporate citizen is likely to change jobs up to eight times in his lifetime and change careers two to three times. At least one of those instances is likely to be an involuntary separation, layoff, RIF, firing… Whatever you want to call it, it is what it is.

The unlikely event of involuntary termination can be a humiliating experience. I have known fellow workers who kept personal items to a minimum in the office for this very reason. After seeing the devastation of a layoff or termination, they did not want to have too many personal items to carry out, much less leave behind.

111

The typical layoff or reduction in force tends to come down fast; affected employees are unexpectedly asked to attend a meeting in an auditorium, conference room, or manager's office. They are generally told together, keeping the explanation consistent. The terminations are usually immediate. The affected employees are usually told that it is not their fault, the company hates to do this, and there was no alternative, and that the company wants to help you.

> ▼ **TIP: In the event of an involuntary termination and you decide to take it up with legal counsel, keep it to yourself. Do not share it with your former co-workers, neighbors, or friends.**

These meetings typically explain any severance pay policies that have been deployed, continuation of benefits, and the attempt the company is willing to go to help you toward re-employment. They usually make it clear that this is a termination. They usually make it clear that the company will not be rehiring anyone. A lot of this is a formality; discrepancies in times like these lead to lawsuits.

During this meeting, you are explained the implication of the termination. If you are offered severance, employers ask in exchange that you sign a document. This document must be explained and in many states a cooling-off period must be offered, allowing the employee time to consider the offer. One item usually contained is the old "no recourse" statement, meaning, in exchange for this consideration (usually payment), you agree to not take action against your previous employer, including keeping your secret information private and away from competitors.

This is time to keep your cool. There will be disappointed people in the room: Some will be cocky, and some will be emotional. This is no time to sign anything. Listen to what they are saying. These mass firings are well planned and thought out. Things you need to know are described, like COBRAs, retirement plans, pensions, and the like.

Expect to see security guards in or around the facility and do not expect to be allowed back to your work area. They might suggest that you bring your briefcase or pocketbook. Expect that your belongings will be inventoried and sent to you quickly. These are trying times. Companies attempt to make this as pleasant a process as they can. They do not want any trouble from you or their remaining employees. This can be a major damper to morale going forward.

The law gives employers a great deal of leeway in deciding whether to fire an employee, but there are limits. If the employee does not have an employment contract and if the employer has never made any promises to the employee about termination, then he can be fired for any reason that isn't illegal.

If the employee has an employment contract or if the employer has made promises to the employee, then that contract or those promises will control when the employee can be fired.

In most cases with an employment contract or where the employer makes promises, he can only fire the employee for something called "good cause."

Productivity Improvement Plans

Productivity plans, PIPs, should be warning enough that the boat is pulling out of the harbor and the company does not expect to see you on it. A PIP becomes necessary when either a flagrant violation of company policy has occurred or the general performance of the employee is sub-par. When a PIP is introduced after a company policy violation that did not warrant immediate termination, there is little warning. Employees with exemplary track records are usually given a PIP to correct a behavior, and the plan might include outside involvement, possible counseling, legal action, or physical rehabilitation. For employees who have not measured up to acceptable performance levels, a PIP should not be unexpected. Corporations generally have documented previous meetings to discuss the performance to avoid the possibility of lengthy legal liability.

Be wary if you find a PIP as reason for termination during a general reduction in force. If you have not received warnings that your performance is not up to par, you might be well served to request, in writing, copies of the documentation on file leading up to the termination. If the supporting documents do not exist, or the company refuses to make them available to you, seek competent employment counsel who specializes in plaintiff matters.

As a rule, the cards are stacked against the employee, whether deserving or not. The manner in which a disciplinary action is recorded and the frequency in which it is revisited can be detrimental when cuts are in order. Usually, when a company takes the time to orchestrate a corrective action, it means business, and a positive remedy is usually impossible to attain. I know of one employee who survived an action plan. One statement was taken out of context, and, had it not been for the seasoned maturity of a company executive, he might have been summarily dismissed. Instead, he was given a six-month probationary period. He was required to file routine written reports documenting his every move, and he was subjected to routine face-to-face discussions with his immediate manager, who showed no sympathy. The purpose of this story is not to tout the miraculous efforts of this individual but to point out that this probation was designed so that the employee would quit. If you are faced with a productivity plan, see if there is a way out. Companies often would be willing to extend a generous severance offer, allowing you time to find employment elsewhere.

Should you decide to take an involuntary termination matter up with an attorney, choose competent counsel. Choose someone who specializes in plaintiff employment matters, meaning he does not represent companies in employment matters. Listen to their counsel; if they say you do not have a case, take heed, get a second opinion if necessary. These types of lawsuits are on the rise but very difficult to prove.

Severance

The law does not require employers to give severance packages to employees who are fired. However, if the employer ever promised the employee a severance package, he should deliver that promise.

A Better Deal on the Way Out

The early retirement offer, sometimes referred to as the "golden handshake," can be sufficient warning that changes are in the wind. Offers of buyouts including health insurance, pension consideration, and the like, need to be taken seriously. Henry Blodgett, an analyst at Merrill Lynch covering dot.com stocks, was offered a $2 million buyout. His decision was easy; he took it. For most employees, the answer is not so clear-cut. Do you grab the money and benefits now, hoping that you will have enough to see you through retirement or another job?

The objective of the company is for enough people to step forward and take the offer to eliminate the need for a layoff. If enough people do not take the offer, well, you know the answer. Younger employees have an easier time making this decision; they tend to find it easier in the job market. Older workers who are closer to retirement find it difficult to make this decision. Often times, decisions involve the dollar amount of monthly pension payments and the number of years left till 59 and 1/2 years of age where 401(k)

> ▼ **TIP: If the unavoidable should happen and your longtime employer is asking you to consider early retirement or face the reality of being terminated, give it serious consideration. If you believe you are due more, ask for it; it cannot hurt and keep it to yourself.**

money can be withdrawn without penalty. Other decisions are more complex, involving health issues for you and your spouse or commitments to children regarding money for educational needs, the amount of money in savings, or the amount of debt.

Older workers will find it harder to locate replacement jobs at or near their previous wages. Employers tend to be looking for longer commitments from higher earning older employees. Often these buyout victims have to settle for lower paying jobs in order to keep working.

Buyouts take on many different forms. Sometimes a buyout includes payment for lost compensation, usually based on years of service, like one to three weeks' pay for each year of service. Also consider whether health insurance, employer 401(k) contributions, or vacation pay is included. Many times employers will re-calculate workers' pensions with accelerated factors yielding higher monthly payments upon eligibility as an inducement. Health insurance benefits until Medicare eligibility make the decision easier but with accelerating health care costs, many buyout offers have caps in these areas.

Be aware of tax implications if your package is a lump-sum payment. Stock options are also another item for consideration. Make sure you understand the implications on a personal level as well as a professional level. Talk to the human resources personnel assigned to the effort. Then speak with your tax professional as well as your investment advisers. These people can offer significant insight into the unknown and help you position your resources and tax consequences to your favor.

The last two items are: make sure you negotiate, and hunt for a new job. Do not be afraid to ask for special consideration. Then get out that résumé, start networking, think about change, tighten your belt, remember your loved ones, because when it's all over, they will be the only ones left for you.

Retirement May be a Better Option Than You Realize

Many people affected by reductions have experienced layoffs

or firings, often times though, retirement can be the answer. Sometimes, these conditions can be coerced by your employer but, usually, the employee stands to benefit from these actions. In the case that you did not decide to depart on your own, you might want to consider retirement.

You might be astonished when you call the Social Security Administration to investigate benefits or inquire as to the cost of insurance coverage to bridge you to Medicare. This scenario can easily happen when someone reaches 62 years of age and has three years to go for Medicare. Retirement seems impossible. But if your company has made several offers of early retirement and does not have enough takers, you may find that the offer goes away and you find yourself caught up in a RIF, downsizing initiative, or layoff. Look hard; those excessive cost considerations can be a heck of a lot more costly when you have been unexpectedly terminated or your position eliminated without any consideration.

Exit Interview

The exit interview can be a resourceful experience, especially in finding another job. Many times, customers of the dismissing company will be interested in hiring those terminated from a supplier or partner. This interview might be in conjunction with learning of the layoff or might happen a day or two later.

Often, this is a time when an interviewer will allow you to say anything that you want. You might be inclined to dump on management or the company in general. Don't do it. This is the time to watch your tongue. Do not conspire with other employees facing the same dilemma. You are likely to be asked about your experience with the company. It is a chance to be honest, but do not volunteer any information. Your bitterness will be discounted and most likely will not have an affect. You might be asked to comment on your direct manager; keep your comments brief and supportive. When asked what you liked about the company, be honest; find something positive to say no matter how bad it hurts. The positive comments might be to an individual who has the power to extend a severance package or possibly hire outside contractors to do the job that was eliminated. Your spouting off about poor treatment will not do you well. *Do not burn bridges*. Be as positive as you can be at this time. Do not gripe or complain, because these interviewers might have leads for you.

References

Generally, all a company will do today is verify dates of employment and possibly the rate of pay upon separation. Generally, companies refrain from commenting about the reason for separation; they defer to company policy as the reason for failing to comment. The company can incur significant liability, so the general guideline is to limit comments. Otherwise the company and possibly the commenter may be vulnerable to a defamation suit from the former employee.

Outplacement Firms

In cases in which restructuring or incompatibility of skill mix requires a change in staff or the elimination of positions, outplacement firms provides both high quality, individualized career transition services and effective interventions for remaining employees, ensuring a continuation of employee productivity, loyalty, and motivation. Their services generally include comprehensive career transition services:

- Outplacement programs for individual and/or group needs
- Career transition consulting
- Job search strategic coaching
- Technology for market research
- Consultation with company representatives prior to notification of employee
- Onsite counseling for affected employees
- Review career strengths, limitations, and preferences, then define career objectives
- Prepare an effective market résumé, biographical overview, and portfolio
- Develop a personal marketing profile with targeted job search strategy

■ Identify primary sources and develop contacts

■ Prioritize industry segment, target list using systematic and targeted networking process

■ Prepare for informational meetings, establish communication strategies with focus on building interview rapport

■ Provide strategic coaching throughout job search

■ Structured job search campaign designed to manage interviewing strategies and negotiate the offer

■ Administrative support including use of an office, computer, fax, copier, e-mail, and Internet access

Your employer is likely to have contracted with an outplacement firm. Your relationship with this firm is generally considered to be confidential. It is important to establish that confidentiality up front, though you will find these firms are usually obligated to report certain facts to the hiring employer.

Choosing the Next Career Step

When the economy takes a downturn, the confidence men come out in force. If you have had the unfortunate luck of losing a job, take time to assess your options. And be careful of any agreements you enter into.

Be wary; there are scams waiting for you. Watch out for those opportunities where you can make big bucks without leaving your home. The old stuffing envelopes scam is a popular one. You are often asked to send in money for startup kits that almost always lead to nothing. Take heed; starting a business or embarking on what you believe is a sure-fire deal can be a mistake.

> ▼ **TIP: Watch out for those opportunities where you can make big bucks without leaving your home.**

Be leery of career counselors who promise you the world. Even good counselors do not claim to have high success rates.

119

The cost can be outrageous, so before you embark down this path, establish some goals and objectives.

Make sure that payments are tagged to milestones. Refrain from retainer fees to be offset by services.

Network marketing or multi-level marketing friends come out of the woodwork. The time of a job loss is not time to take a 180-degree turn in your career; if you have not been in a sales-oriented environment before, do you think that this is the time you'll be successful? You may hear success stories, such as the football coach turned investment counselor who has made a million bucks in the past nine months, the down-and-out housewife who builds a multi-million dollar cosmetics line, or the itinerant preacher who makes his mark in pots and pans. Make sure you know what you're getting into. Some opportunities are better than others. Look at the facts: 3 percent of multi-level marketing members earn in excess of $20,000, according to the Direct Sales Association.

The usual approach to direct marketing or network marketing opportunities comes from a well-meaning friend. Take the time to compare several companies; make sure you are being recruited for the right reason. A lot of companies have failed in business because their primary focus was recruiting people in the organization rather than the sale of products or services—the primary reason for commerce. Just belonging to someone's down line is likely to reward everyone other than you; remember, nothing comes free. Look at the company's training plan; make sure it's there and not just based on numerous claims of miracles using their products.

When you have convinced yourself that this is right for you, choose wisely. The failure rates are high but, on the other hand, can be very rewarding, both personally and financially.

Many employees of companies in decline, through no fault of their own, are left holding the bag as they begin their spiral downward. Many younger employees are able to make an easy transition to other companies; older workers have a difficult time adjusting to new organizations, the new marketplace, and the new pace of doing business. These hard-working people tend to have a good grasp of their personal needs but tend to falter in information gathering and strategy setting departments. Regardless of your age, keep your skills up to date.

Conclusion

We have danced through the blinding process of assessing where you are in a career, where is your employer, what you can do to change things as well as what you should be doing to secure your future. There are those things that you are in complete control of, day in and day out, and then there are those factors that you can only prepare for. You have to be ready for the inevitable, carefully measuring each step and weighing all the odds. This book has attempted to prepare you on several fronts; now it is time to accept the inevitable. You must be prepared for that next job.

Put in play several strategies that will keep you positioned for change. Finding that next job is often easier when you are working than not. Many times it's not what you know but rather who you know that counts the most. Maintain that pipeline of opportunities as well as that close network of friends and associates who can help compress the time between jobs or speed the process of finding a job if currently unemployed. After all the concept of "Six Degrees of Separation" speaks volumes here.

While preparing for and engaging in the process of changing employers, have a clear-cut set of goals and objectives. Consider those things you deem important to your family and yourself. You need to maintain a sense of protocol and etiquette as you go about the business at hand. Understand that you are reaching "free agent" status with each move. There are many factors to consider in a job change or loss as well as a career change. Plan your move, if possible; if not, be professional about it. Make a full-time job of looking for a job. Wake up every morning with the intent that this is the day.

You may very well find that this is a time to consider non-permanent full-time employment. You might find that consulting could be your chance to take your current skill set and apply it to a new industry, possibly one that might be in favor over your usual and customary career field. Think through your options; be creative in your career search. This might be the time to consider

121

self-employment, securing a franchise, or developing several part-time permanent jobs. You might be tempted to cash in your life savings or retirement to achieve some goal you might have dreamed of for years. Proceed with caution; too many well-suspecting people have lost considerable sums or their money as well as that of friends and family living a dream. *Be careful!*

Survival Tips

■ Maintain contact with peers outside your place of employment, possibly through trade or professional associations as well as local service organizations.

■ Plan your career moves as much as possible.

■ If left without a job, pursue a new one on a full-time basis.

■ Be courteous and follow up as promised when networking for employment or a job change.

Questions for Consideration

■ Have you considered your "free agent" status?

■ Are you planning your next move now or have you become complacent?

▼

The Survivability Quotient

If you're like most people, you attempted to complete the SQ prior to reading the book, only to come up very disappointed with your score. No problem. Reading the book is likely to improve your score 5 to 10 percent because then you're more aware of your weaknesses and have some ideas how to improve in those areas.

While there are countless variables in our jobs, lives, and careers that we could measure objectively, we have carefully chosen those that are very relevant to today's economy. The book was designed to take the most important factors in your career—the ones you have control over as well as those you can do nothing about—and make them relevant. The SQ takes that relevance to another level in you being able to quantify your feelings and knowledge on that topic.

Each section of the SQ corresponds to the same section of the book, while it might not map directly to the text. The book is designed to point out those variables worthy of consideration that will either help you do a more complete job or prepare you for the unforeseen obstacle.

Employment in the 21st century is returning to that of our forefathers; there will be plenty of work, just not necessarily permanent and full time. The SQ is designed to be your measuring stick. Each section will calculate its own percentage. This calculation should provide evidence about the things you should be paying attention to. A low score in an area might suggest seeking counsel from a friend, coworker, spouse/significant other, partner, professional employment coach, support group, or counselor. These are your scores, not the author's. You have the opportunity to take this quick exam as often as you like. It is recommended that you take it at least quarterly. While the SQ was conveniently placed in the back of the book for a self-score, it is also available in a slightly different format at the website www.corpsurvival.com. You are welcome to change the variables if you choose, but be consistent when you score yourself.

Take into account your physical mood and the current attitude toward your job or career. It is recommended that you take the SQ under different conditions; for instance, just following a great day at work and then possibly a day when you are at your worst. Look for the variances in the scores; some will never change, others will change drastically. Attempt to understand the differences and what you can do to improve or sustain the change. Remember, the objective is to go up.

The SQ is laid out in sections and in each section we address the most relevant conditions affecting your career in that area. Some conditions allow for only one selection. Others allow you to select all that apply. This is important and should be obvious. Choose carefully; in some instances a bit of research might be necessary. Whatever the case, follow the guidelines.

The results should be your yardstick for your present job or career as well as the survivability of your employer. Take the time to think about these issues. Your score should be fairly confidential. We suggest keeping your results to yourself. Do not make this everyone's business. If you decide that additional education and certification might be necessary to improve a section score, make plans to do it; just do not make it everyone's business.

As for the scoring, be honest and realistic, and do not be surprised at your outcome. I did not attempt to score myself until I was almost finished with the book. I suspected I was capable of getting a solid 80 percent. Much to my surprise, having seen my employer at the time go through round one of a series of layoffs, I scored a 53, far from 80 percent. This obviously skewed the score a bit, but it was not the additional 27 percent I was expecting.

Your analysis of each section, as well as your overall score, should allow for 10 percent wiggle room, but here are the suggestions:

40 percent and under: This score indicates a severe deficiency. You can expect to have possibly one section with this score in your SQ. This should be a good indicator as to what you should be working on. You might want to seek the assistance of a trained professional to address these issues, likely a career coach or counselor.

41 percent to 60 percent: This is considered average. You can expect that there will be obvious conditions that need addressing. Take the time to do some planning in your career or personal life. Don't attempt to do it in one sitting. Begin to incorporate improving those conditions in your way of life. Possibly look for an outside group for professional networking or a community-based organization that offers continual education, training, and counseling.

61 percent to 80 percent: You are in the upper percentiles. You are likely to be spending a good deal of time planning and evaluating your life and career. You should be devoting time to coaching or mentoring others, possibly within your current employer or through a non-profit organization like a church or service organization. Having a high score does not mean that you can drop your guard; look for the areas of deficiency, those places where you can possibly experience a dip in percentage. Things to look for are in the areas of personal finance and the health and well-being of your employer.

81 percent to 100 percent. There is a good chance that you have made a mistake in calculating your score. Look over the numbers again. Part of Section One requires you to subtract Part B. If you find you have still excelled, put the book down, wait a few weeks and try it again. If you still pass with flying colors, put down the book, pick up a pen; workers in Corporate America are starved for good content that will improve their lives. Write a book, go on the road, and share your talent.

You have reached that point, go for it, you have nothing to lose. If you have not read the book, do yourself a favor and read it. If you still choose not to read the book, I thank you for buying the book. You might want to visit my website, www.corpsurvival.com, and have access to the SQ for continued scoring.

Survivability Quotient

Section 1A: Today's Corporate Climate
Assess the impact of major business trends

Enter Score Here

Present employer's organizational structure (select one)

Privately held	4
Family Owned	3
Partnership	2
Employee owned	3
Publicly traded US (NYSE, American or NASDAQ)	4
Publicly Traded ADR (NYSE, American or NASDAQ)	3
Publicly traded (other exchange)	2
Wholly owned subsidiary	2
Public partnership	2

(Total points possible: 4)

Rate your company's ability to remain in present ranking (select one)

Sector ranking will increase	4
Sector ranking will remain the same	2
Sector ranking will decrease	1

(Total points possible: 4)

Rank your operational division or department (select only one, use discretion, think hard)

Most valued, operationally sound, profitable, first-place position with company	4
Mildly profitable, adheres to mainstream business model, clearly not first-place	3
Viable unit, capable of being profitable within 12-18 months	2
Other	1

(Total points possible: 4)

Insight on unit's long term viability (select all that apply)

Unit is aligned with core business model   2
Unit represents the the most growth opportunity
       over other division   2
Leadership/management of unit is on the inside
       of the executive management team   1
(Total points possible: 5)

Section 1A Total Points (17 points possible)

Your score as percentage of 17 possible points

Section 1B: Signs of Things to Come (This amount will be subtracted)

Mergers (select all that apply)

Your employer has engaged in an industry
       merger over the past year   1
Your company's leadership remained
       in charge after a merger   1
The merged company's management took the
       leadership position   2
The leadership of the merged entity has
       changed in past 6 months   2
(Total points possible: 3)

Acquisitions (select all that apply)

Your employer has been involved in an
       industry merger over the past 2 years   2
Your company was the acquirer   1
Your company was acquired   2
You joined your company post-acquisition   1
     (Total points possible: 3)

Spinoffs (select all that apply)

Your company has spun off a significant
business unit in the past 3 years   1

Any of those divested business units have
experienced reductions in force   2

You are part of a divested entity   1

The leadership of the divested entity has
changed in past 9 months   2

(Total points possible: 3)

Management change (select all that apply)

Executive level   1
Upper management   2
Direct manager or supervisor   2
Audit firm   1
(Total points possible: 3)

Section 1B Total Points (12 Points Possible)
(This section will be subtracted)

Your score as percentage of 12 possible points

Section 2: Evaluating the Health of Your Employer

Perception of your present employer's stock price if publicly traded

Performing well   4
Performing marginally   2
Performing negatively   1
(Total points possible: 4)

Perception of the value of your company if privately held

Performing well   4
Performing marginally   2
Performing negatively   1
(Total points possible: 4)

Cash on hand select (select only two)

Improved over past reporting period	quarterly	3
	annually	4
Same as past reporting period	quarterly	2
	annually	2
Less than past reporting period	quarterly	0
	annually	0

(Total points possible: 7)

Recent management statements to analyst and 10K/Q filings

Positive	3
Marginal	1
Negative	0

(Total points possible: 3)

Company's profitablity (select all that apply)

Improved over past reporting period	quarterly	3
	annually	4
Same as past reporting period	quarterly	2
	annually	2
Less than past reporting period	quarterly	0
	annually	0

(Total points possible: 7)

Section 2 Total Points (25 Points Possible)

Your score as percentage of 25 possible points

Section 3A: Evaluating Your Corporate Value

Level of completed education (select one)

High school diploma   1
Technical Certificate   3
Associate of arts degree   3
Bachelor's Degree   4
Graduate degree (consider being overvalued)   3
(Total points possible: 4)

Skill enhancement activity (select all that apply)

Foreign language   2
Skill certification   2
Utilizing tuition reimbursement program   1
(Total points possible: 5)

Networking activities (select all that apply)

Trade association membership   1
Professional association membership   1
Social organizations   1
Unions   1
Trade show events   1
Independent networking association   1
(Total points possible: 3)

Section 3A Total Points (12 Possible Points)

Your score as percentage of 12 possible points

Section 3B: Assessing Your Present Value

Select your current position (select one)

Clerical	2
Semi-skilled labor	2
Skilled labor with certification	3
Degreed	2
Professional	3
Middle management	2
Upper management	3
Executive	4

(Total points possible: 4)

Years of service with your current employer (select one)

1-3 years	2
3-7 years	4
7-15 years	3
15+ years	3

(Total points possible: 4)

Most recent evaluation or review (select one)

Top 10%	4
Positive finish	3
Middle of the road	2
Needs improvement	1

(Total points possible: 4)

Last promotion (select one)

Not applicable	3
Within year	4
1-2 years	3
3-5 years	2
5+ years	2
None	1

(Total points possible: 4)

Section 3B Total Points (16 Points Possible)

Your score as percentage of 16 possible points

Section 4: Creating a Lifelong Career Plan

Knowledge of your rights (select all that apply)

Knowledge of benefits offered by your current
    employer   2
Knowledge of harassment and discrimination
    issues   1
(Total points possible: 3)

Effects of aging (select all that apply)

Hobbies   1
Outward appearance   2
Overall health   1
(Total points possible: 4)

Location on the earnings curve (select one)

Early entrant   3
Midway   4
Peak   2
Downward trending   2
(Total points possible: 4)

Susceptibility to future trends (select all that apply)

Conducive to working remote   1
Ability to readily adapt to technology   1
Technical certification required   1
Non-dependent on oil   1
Multinational skills   1
Health-related   1
(Total points possible: 4)

Section 4 Total Points (15 Points Possible)

Your score as percentage of 15 possible points

Section 5: Engaging the Right Investment Adviser

Legal (select all that apply): Do you have...
Will/trust   1
Living will   1
Durable power of attorney   1
Organ donor   1
  (Total points possible: 4)

Insurance (select all that apply)
Private term life insurance   1
Maximum company-sponsored life   1
Mortgage protection insurance   1
  (Total points possible: 3)

Financial (select all that apply)
Credit card debt less than 10% of salary   2
Rainy day fund of 6-months salary   2
Fully funded educational account (529,
          pre-paid college)   1
Value of less than of the years left on mortgage
   divided by years to retirement (62, 65, 66)   2
401(k) or 403(b) or thrift savings account,
          company sponsored (maintaining at
          least 50% contribution)   2
Individual IRA   2
Other   1
  (Total points possible: 12)

Section 5 Total Points (19 Points Possible)I

Your score as percentage of 19 possible points

Section 6: Planning Your Next Job
Skills and qualifications (select all that apply)

You have a current résumé	2
Latest documented personal skills assessment	2
Last time you spoke with potential references	1
Have discussed your career with a recruiter (head hunter) in the past 9 months	1
Attended trade/industry association meeting in past 180 days	1
Had contact with an individual in your industry within past 30 days (outside present company)	2
Affiliated with an outside independent networking organization	2
Section 6 Total Points (7 Points Possible)	

Your score as percentage of 7 possible points

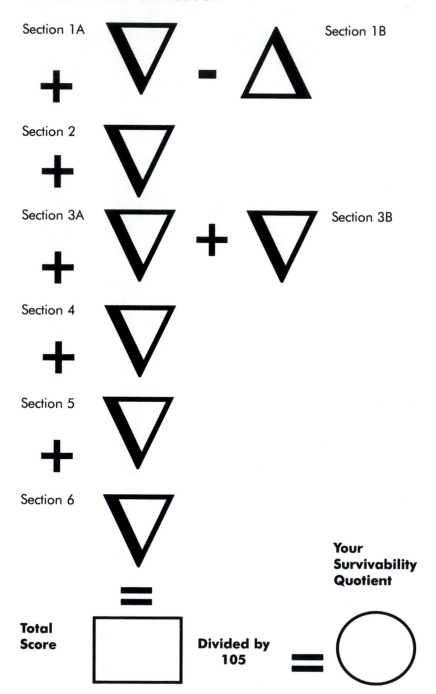

Section 1A

Section 1B

Section 2

Section 3A

Section 3B

Section 4

Section 5

Section 6

Your Survivability Quotient

Total Score

Divided by 105

▼

Discrimination and Termination

In the 25- to 54-year old age group, there is a growing segment of our corporate labor force that crosses the delicate 40-year-old line. There are laws that offer protection for this over-40 segment of the workforce. This segment can expect special treatment, whether they actually see it or not. Any company that discriminates against or terminates an employee age 40 or older will face the potential liability of an unwanted lawsuit if it fails to proceed with caution. Expect most employers to have followed the book. It's usually the undocumented termination of a single individual that draws legal attention or a large-scale layoff, in which a specific group of people feel as though they were dealt with unfairly.

Discrimination

Discrimination occurs when an employer treats someone differently on the basis of some characteristic, such as age, race, gender, hair color, height, and so on. Although some forms of discrimination are perfectly legal, discrimination without cause is illegal. In 1964, Congress enacted the Age Discrimination in Employment Act (ADEA) and Title VII of the Civil Rights Act to eliminate employment discrimination. In 1991, the Title VII law was amended to overturn the effects of several Supreme Court decisions regarding discrimination. Today, only certain companies are liable for discrimination and harassment under the provisions of Title VII. Those employers must have 15 or more employees for each working day of 20 or more calendar weeks of the year of the act or the preceding year. While these limits are offered through federal law, most states do not offer such limitations. If you believe you have been discriminated against, seek professional legal help. Seek a law firm that specializes in employment lawsuits representing plaintiffs (the employee).

■ Legal Forms of Discrimination

There are instances where discrimination is legal and legitimate. Take the example of the position of firefighter. The job certainly would require that an individual applying for the job be able to pick up a certain weight, let's say 150 pounds. This might not be possible for a woman, or someone who is disabled or slight of frame.

■ Illegal Forms of Discrimination

If a characteristic is specifically listed in an anti-discrimination law, then it is illegal to discriminate against someone on the basis of that characteristic. Federal law prohibits discrimination on the basis of race, gender, pregnancy, national origin (including affiliation with a Native American tribe), religion, disability, and age (if the person is at least 40 years old). State and local laws often prohibit additional types of discrimination, including discrimination on the basis of marriage, sexual orientation, and weight. To learn more about your state and local laws, contact your state Department of Labor or your state Fair Labor Employment Office.

■ Age Discrimination

By now all employers know better than to be found guilty of age discrimination. The law is intended to protect workers age 40 and older from discrimination on the basis of being "too old." Wrongful termination calls for the employee to prove that the dismissal was unlawful.

Older workers often find emerging industries as challenging. The bright young individuals who dominate certain industries make it difficult for older workers to be noticed. The youth tend to claim new ideas and fresh approaches while the older worker brings balance to the organization.

The older worker who is wrongfully excluded has rights not to be set aside. Make sure that older personnel are considered and included in all important activities. It is illegal to force older employees out of the workforce through negative changes in their performance evaluation or even pressuring them to take early retirement through financial incentives. Policies that are formed should include equal access for older workers, such as on-the-job education and career development, as well as promotional oppor-tunities. Make sure that "pre-retirement moves" of younger personnel have not occurred in which assumptions are made about older workers' plans for retire-ment.

> ▼ **TIP: Make sure that older personnel are considered and included in all important activities.**

These flawed corpo-rate cultures have been the demise of many a good corporation. The cost of mistreating older workers is on the rise, whether an out-of-court settlement is agreed to or a full-fledged court case ensues. Between 1988 and 1995, people claiming dis-crimination were awarded an average of $219,000. An older work-er who is discharged is not as likely to be rehired at the same rate of pay and comparable position, therefore damages for future lost wages will weigh heavily. In age discrimination cases, the employ-ee can sue for a variety of things, including emotional distress and punitive damages. The age discrimination lawsuit has the poten-tial to have a significantly higher award than any other discrimi-nation case.

Please make sure that you are justified in your evidence that you have been discriminated against. Then seek out professional advice. Do the math; it might not be worth your while. If you have a trade association or labor union, you might want to pursue this venue without considering a legal fight. The process is not a bed of roses; it will be arduous. Seek competent counsel, gain favor from your family and do not, I repeat, do not discuss this with anyone but your attorney.

■ Other Discriminations

Employers cannot terminate employees on the basis of age, race, national origin, disability or if the employee was a whistle blower. Whistle blowing is when an employee turns in an employer for illegal activities. An employer can terminate a woman who is more than 40 years of age, pregnant, walks with a limp, black, Hindu, and lesbian. The employer cannot terminate that individual for being a woman, for being more than 40, for expecting a child, for being black, for practicing the Hindu faith, and for having a same gender sexual orientation. Watch the language here; they can be let go but not because of who they are. If you believe you have been wrongfully terminated, seek the advice of a professional, an attorney who specializes in employment law and favors plaintiff actions. One who has experience on the other side of the table is a plus but not necessary.

Harassment

Harassment is a type of discrimination. The same laws that prohibit discrimination on the basis of protected characteristics (such as race, gender, religion, and so on) also prohibit harassment on the basis of those characteristics. Harassment occurs when an employee or group of employees must endure a work environment that is hostile, offensive, or intimidating to them because they have a protected characteristic.

Harassing conduct includes such actions as:
■ Moniker
■ Ridicule
■ Humiliating jokes and graphic depictions
■ Implied and overt fear of hostility

Sexual Harassment

Sexual harassment is a type of gender discrimination. It is any unwelcome sexual advance or conduct on the job that creates a daunting, antagonistic, or disgusting working environment. It is any distasteful conduct related to an employee's gender that a reasonable woman or man should not have to endure.

■ Sexual Harassment Recourse

Notify your manager or supervisor immediately. Should your manager be the offending party, notify personnel immediately. The following process will be thorough and complete. Make sure that you have your facts, including evidence, dates, times, actions etc. The complaint will be taken seriously. This will anger many people, including people who once were your friends. There will be allegations brought against the whistle blower; remember, you are protected. Many times, employers have a no-fault policy when dealing with sexual harassment. They tend to exercise the "at will" clause and terminate the offending party if there is the slightest suspicion of evidence.

■ Can I Be Fired for Blowing the Whistle?

Absolutely not, most anti-discrimination laws—state and federal—contain a provision that forbids employers from retaliation against employees who assert their rights to a workplace free of discrimination. Firing and disciplinary actions constitute retaliation and offer serious liability to the employer. Expect special treatment and considerations while a company investigates claims of discrimination or sexual harassment.

Wrongful Termination

Wrongful termination is the right of an employee to sue his employer for damages (loss of wage and "fringe" benefits, and, if against "public policy," for punitive damages). To bring such a suit, the discharge of the employee must have been without "cause," and the employee:

■ Had an express contract of continued employment or there was an "implied" contract based on the circumstances of his/her hiring or legitimate reasons to believe the employment would be permanent

■ There is a violation of statutory prohibitions against discrimination due to race, gender, sexual preference, or age, or

■ The discharge was contrary to "public policy" such as in retribution for exposing dishonest acts of the employer.

An employee who believes he has been wrongfully terminated may bring an action (file a suit) for damages for discharge, as well as for breach of contract, but court decisions have become increasingly strict in limiting an employee's grounds for suit.

Mediation and arbitration

So you signed a document upon starting employment agreeing to use mediation or arbitration as a means of settling any claims of unfair practices brought by the employee against the employer, reconsideration of an employee evaluation, remedy for unjust·termination or improved explanation of a loosely worded policy. There is a difference between mediation and arbitration; it's important to know what you might have signed up for.

A mediator normally has no authority to render a decision; it's up to the parties themselves to work informally toward their own agreement. The mediator is there to facilitate the process and offer consolation when necessary. An arbitrator, on the other hand, administers a contested hearing between the parties and then, acting as a judge, rends a legally binding decision. The arbitrator's decision-making power may, however, be limited based on a written agreement between the parties. For example, the parties may agree that damages will be awarded within a given amount. Arbitration, which has long been used to resolve commercial and labor disputes, might even resemble a court hearing—with testimony of witnesses and evidence submission. Understand what you have signed. Many times employers even go so far as to suggest the mediation or arbitration firm to be used in the event of a dispute, seriously tipping the scales in their favor.

Litigation

I believe all avenues should be exhausted before using legal action in a dispute with a former employer. Most employers do not want a lawsuit and will generally do whatever is necessary to avoid litigation. However, there are instances where a person's rights were violated, or a group of people's rights have been violated, to the point at which legal representation is necessary. It usually does not cost anything to visit with a lawyer on an employment matter. See several attorneys or law firms that specialize in these matters on the plaintiff's side. If you have been financially devastated by an employer dispute, there are instances where no cost representation is available to you. Here are several situations in which you may be able to get an attorney to represent you for free:

■ If you've been injured.

If you have been severely injured and wish to sue, a lawyer may agree to represent you on a "contingency fee" basis. This means that you pay attorney's fees only when and if the attorney recovers money for you; the attorney takes an agreed-upon percentage of that money as fees.

Be aware, however, that even if a lawyer takes your case on a contingency fee basis, you still have to pay costs, which can add up to several thousand dollars. Costs include court filing fees, court reporters' fees, expert witnesses, and jury fees. The good news is that if you win your case, the judge will usually order your adversary to pay you back for these costs.

■ If you qualify for legal aid.

If you can't afford an attorney, you may qualify for legal aid. Legal aid lawyers are government lawyers who represent people with low incomes in a variety of legal situations, including eviction defense, denial of unemployment compensation or other benefits, and consumer credit problems. If you think you might qualify, look in your telephone directory or ask a local attorney, lawyer referral service or elected representative for the nearest legal aid office.

■ If your claim involves an issue of social justice.

If your dispute involves a social justice issue, an attorney with an interest in that issue may represent you on a "pro bono""(no fee or reduced fee) basis. For example, if your claim involves sexual harassment by an employer, abuse by a spouse or partner, discrimination in housing or employment, freedom of speech or religion, or environmental pollution, you may find an attorney or organization willing to represent you pro bono. Call a local bar association or a private organization that deals with the kind of problem you face, such as the American Civil Liberties Union, the NAACP Legal Defense Fund, the Natural Resources Defense Council, the National Women's Law Center, or the Lambda Legal Defense and Education Fund (gay and lesbian rights).

■ **If you face criminal charges.**

If you've been charged with a crime and cannot afford to hire your own lawyer, you have a constitutional right to an attorney at government expense. At your request, an attorney, often from a public defender's office, can be appointed to represent you when you are formally charged in court with a criminal offense.

Class Action

The last point about this topic pertains to the groups of individuals who believe their rights have been violated. There are law firms that specialize in getting large groups of people together for the benefit of righting a wrong. The Blockbuster Video class action lawsuit offers a good example. Customers who were overcharged late fees on videos received coupons for discounted or free rentals while the attorneys counted the real money in this lawsuit.

Class action is a type of lawsuit in which one or several people can sue on behalf of a larger group of people. Several examples exist of appropriate class action suits: employees of a corporation who have suffered from a pattern of age, sex, or racial discrimination; homeowners near an environmental hazard caused by a person or corporation; consumers who purchased faulty products; patients prescribed certain medicines; merchants and consumers who were overcharged for products or services; and, lastly, investors who were victimized. Not every class action lawsuit has a happy ending. If there is a way to hold down the size of the group, you might have a good chance; just watch out for the sharks in flannel suits.

More often than not, defense and plaintiff counsel are seen as the predators, ringing up high hourly fees on the defense side or taking astoundingly high percentages representing the interest of the group as a whole. Far too often, the attorneys are the big winners, and the effective parties see little to nothing from the outcome. Before you engage in a class action suit, make sure you have considered your personal stake and whether there is a remote possibility of succeeding individually. Then when you are satisfied that the government is unable to protect your interest sufficiently, you should seek out competent counsel who specializes in this type of litigation. Expect that it will take a long time and the outcome might be dynamic but have little to no effect on your pocket book.

▼

Occupational Facts

The following numbers are courtesy of the U.S. Bureau of Labor Statistics, 2000.

Estimate of Employment and Mean Annual Wage for Major Occupational Groups

Industry Segment	Total Employment	Mean Annual Mean Wage
Management	7,782,680	$68,190
Business and Finance Operations	4,619,270	$48,470
Computer and Mathematical	2,932,810	$58,050
Architecture Engineering	2,575,620	$54,060
Life, Physical, and Social Sciences	1,038,670	$47,790
Community and Social Services	1,469,000	$32,910
Legal	890,910	$68,930
Education, Training, and Library	7,450,860	$37,900
Arts, Entertainment, Design, Sports, and Media	1,513,420	$38,640
Healthcare Practitioners and Technical	6,041,210	$47,990
Healthcare Support	3,039,430	$21,040
Protective Services	3,009,070	$30,780
Food Preparation and Serving	9,955,060	$16,070
Building Maintenance and Groundskeeping	4,318,070	$19,750
Personal Care and Services	2,700,510	$20,150

Industry Segment	Total Employment	Mean Annual Mean Wage
Sales and Related	13,506,880	$27,990
Office Administration and Support	22,936,140	$26,300
Farming, Fishing, and Forestry	460,700	$18,860
Construction and Extraction	6,187,360	$34,440
Installation, Maintenance, and Repair	5,318,490	$33,760
Production	12,400,080	$26,450
Transportation and Material Moving	9,592,740	$25,630

Let Us Hear From You

Tell us how the Corporate Survival Handbook has helped you. Send your feedback to:

Steve Isler
www.corpsurvival.com.

Additional copies of this book also are available at the website: www.corpsurvival.com.